Sense, Sensibility and Sensation:

The Marvelous Miniatures and
Perfect Pastels of Laura Coombs Hills

America's Lyrical Impressionist

Diane Elizabeth Kelleher

authorHOUSE

AuthorHouse™
1663 Liberty Drive
Bloomington, IN 47403
www.authorhouse.com
Phone: 833-262-8899

Published by AuthorHouse 05/10/2023

ISBN: 979-8-8230-0805-1 (sc)
ISBN: 979-8-8230-0804-4 (e)

Library of Congress Control Number: 2023908538

Print information available on the last page.

Any people depicted in stock imagery provided by Getty Images are models,
and such images are being used for illustrative purposes only.
Certain stock imagery © Getty Images.

This book is printed on acid-free paper.

Contents

For my Mother, Hildur Englund Kelleher (1921-2004)

Note to the Reader

Prior to the rise of Modernism, developments in English literature sometimes preceded and portended literary innovations in America. And, American literature often reflected broader cultural constructs which surfaced in the pictorial arts. Thus, with the confluence of these two occurrences, it seems plausible that the two types of literature and the development of miniatures exhibited somewhat parallel destinies.

To explore the Hills narrative is to adhere in part to an atypical historical framework centered upon the notions of Sense, Sensibility and Sensation. Essentially then, this broad approach is founded, not upon typical art historical causation, but rather coincidences which function to inform our overall understanding of Hills' philosophical traditions. These ideas prove to be, not to the exclusion of typical art historical information, but merely an adjunct to it.

Thus, the framework for this book of Sense, Sensibility and Sensation, reflects less of an interest in factors of actual, direct causation, than those of simple coincidence and is in this sense, in some areas, hence, somewhat speculative in orientation.

For example, there is no actual causal relationship which can be proved between Hills' miniatures of ladies and English poetry. (We only *know* from words expressed in her own letters that Hills read books by Florence Thompson: She may or may not have read Shelley, Byron, or other English poets.) Yet there *are* similarities of sensibility between her lovely miniature portrayals of women and the emotional tone of the poets that can function to inform our understanding of the essence of Hills and her work.

So, we will consider answers to the questions: What are the philosophical (literary and cultural) traditions out of which Hills' art arises? And: What is the art historical nature of her art?

A response to the initial query involves mention of the roles played by empiricism, lyricism, contemplative Romanticism, and individualism. Respectively, this viewpoint includes: the mention of the influence of colonial literature, Walt Whitman's ideology; the English "Romance poets" - Shelley, Byron and their Italian predecessor

Wyatt; Edmund Burke's idea of beauty, an aesthetic response and contemplative Romanticism; and the changing concept of the individual surrounding Sigmund Freud and psychological modernism.

Exploration of our second question, encompasses facets of Hills' own biography, and a number of facts and ideas proposed by Maryann Sudnick Gunderson in her 2003 thesis: *Dismissed yet Disarming: The Portrait Miniature Revival, 1890-1930.* Naturally, we will also glance precisely at the exact words and thoughts of Hills' contemporary critics.

The final section of this investigation presents discussion devoted to the sensations of color and sensational nature of Hills' pastels and the interplay of Impressionism, color theory, and the regionalism of "Boston Impressionism" in New England.

Moreover, it is hoped that this novel approach will further a fuller understanding of the Laura Coombs Hills narrative, and its place in and contribution to history. It is for this reason that this atypical, tripartite framework was adopted.

Introduction

Celebrated throughout her long lifetime, Laura Coombs Hills and the art she created have yet to receive the serious artistic consideration that they have long deserved. As a portrait miniaturist and floral pastelist, Hills stands at the crossroads with both hands open, fingertips ready to cull distinct artistic values from the roots of three cultural traditions - American, French and English, which by their coexistence and stylistic merger at a particular moment in aesthetic history, speak to Hills' ability to reflect the uniqueness of the past, while holding open for the mere beckoning, the aesthetic place card of the future.

Born in 1859, prior to the Civil War and at the apex of the nation's most fervent stirrings of the forces of simmering feminism, Hills came of age as an artist during the height of the importation of Impressionist incantations prevalent in the 1880s, and as such straddles multiple historical legacies: some as insist upon lingering, some as stand poised to emerge.

Although nearly a generation older than another artist with whom she exhibited, Hills' personality and work nevertheless share with the younger, America's Linear Impressionist, Lilian Westcott Hale, such underlying tenets as simultaneously unite and differentiate both distinguished artists as two of the finest exemplars of the Boston area's uniquely beautiful art, each being a highly individualistic innovator, entrepreneurial feminist, and eloquent practitioner of the best this Nation had to offer.

If the art of Hale spoke to paradox, beauty, and personality, then in derivation, iconographic content, and style, the American art of Laura Coombs Hills embodies duality and a sort of blended polarity between the abstraction of sensation and the realities of empiricism. Hills' art is inherently at times English and French. It is always deeply American. It's elusions are to the orderly processes of reason, natural and civil law; the heartfelt experiences of romance, sentiment, and God; the science of sensation; Naturalism, Regionalism and Impressionism. Here, sense, sensibility and sensation are stylistically intertwined by the unifying force of an additional factor which all of Hills' work shares - the poetics of Lyricism.

Sense, sensibility and sensation: these are the unspoken themes inherent in Laura Coombs Hills' portrait miniatures and floral pastels. Still, what do these three synoptic epithets mean, and why should we wish to study Hills' *oeuvre*? Here, sense is empowered to indicate empirical verisimilitude, or objective truth to that which is seen. Sensibility implies sensitivity to emotion, and to its miniaturistic visage. And sensation heralds the carefully coloristic orchestration of the presentation of an optical symphony of hues.

While these three themes are characteristic of all of Hills' work, each theme is relatively more prominent and pronounced in Hills' different artistic genres. Sense is pronounced in both miniatures and pastels. Sensibility is evident in the romantic nature of her miniatures, and the idea of sensation is most clearly orchestrated in Hills' flower pastels

Still, Hills' contribution to America's art historical traditions is comprised of even more factors. Hills is the arbiter of various legacies including being: (1) the transmitter of nineteenth century Chevreulian color theory to New England's art scene; (2) the exemplar of the earlier, American art tradition of the art-journalist of empiricism; (3) a conduit of American practices relative to the perpetuation of French Impressionism; (4) the perpetuator of an evolved type of American miniature; (5) the intense popularizer of pastels; and (6) finally, the creator of altogether new traditions in American art.

Moreover, Hills' sensational, melodious, enchanting and symphonic use of color in her pastels of flowers and her miniatures on ivory, and the simmering sense of anecdotal emotion pervading her elegant and gentle, romantic images of Newburyporters portrayed in her miniatures, and the aesthetic response all of these works arouse in the viewer, make of Hills a unique and special phenomenon, an artist who occupies a singular place in New England's and indeed the whole of American art, American social history, and American culture. Indeed, since in Hills' exemplary *oeuvre*, sense, sensibility and sensation share the common bond of lyricism, we may refer to Laura Coombs Hills as "America's Lyrical Impressionist".

But what precisely do we mean by lyricism and how is it evident in Hills' *oeuvre*? Several definitions of lyricism are applicable here. Lyricism is the "character and quality of subjectivity and sensuality of expression especially in the arts"[1]; "the quality or state of being melodious"[2]; "having the form and musical quality of a song and especially the character of a songlike outpouring of the poet's own thoughts"[3] or feelings; "the beautiful expression of personal thoughts and feelings in writing or music"[4]; "beautifully full of emotion"[5] as in an aesthetic response; or "a gentle or romantic emotion"[6],[7] Or perhaps most *apropos*, lyrical means having an artistically beautiful or expressive quality.

Hills' art forms are both lyric and lyrical. In the aesthetic response they create, they translate the qualities of one art form, poetry and literature, into those of another art form, the pictorial arts. Both her biographical miniatures and her floral pastels comprise theatrically dramatic monologues wherein the speaker (Hills) addresses a specific person in the audience (the viewer). We term her work, especially her portraits in miniature, lyric since they are, as in literature, a formal type of poetry which expresses personal emotions or feelings, as well as concepts of solitude and beauty.

We term her work lyrical because as lyrical poems are often popular for their musical quality and rhythm and are pleasing to the ear while demonstrating specific moods or emotions through words, Hills' floral pastels in particular constitute well orchestrated harmonies of color. Hills' pastels, as examples of aesthetic lyricism, exist as color induced studies in effusive joy and elation with the identities of each species singing out its individual notes, loudly and clearly in a melodic symphony of color.

Thus, lyricism, here, is meant to encompass not merely the usual reference only to works of music and poetry, but Art as well, for as Hills' work demonstrates, all the Arts can share the same qualities of lyricism.

Indeed, the quality of aesthetic lyricism embedded within Hills' American Impressionist style explains several mysteries, for example: Why, as we gaze upon the ivory miniatures of women painted by Hills do we associate with them the love sonnets addressed to the inamorata of Lord Byron, such as his "Ode to a Lady", or William Wordsworth's "She Was a Phantom of Delight", or Percy Byssche Shelley's "Love's Philosophy" or Hartley Coleridge's "She Is Not Fair"; or even the escapades of heroines peopling the novels of Henry James (such as *Daisy Miller, The Ambassadors,* and *The American*) who traveled abroad as did many of Hills' friends and patrons?

Why, as we look at her early miniatures of men, do we think of the earlier American Colonial miniaturists and their work, such as Benjamin Trott's "Lewis Adams", Walter Robertson's "Augustus Vallette Van Horne", Charles Fraser's "Powell McRae, Nathaniel Rogers' "Man in a Black Coat", Pierre Henri's "James Stanarne or John Deas", or Henry Williams' "Edward Coberly"? Why does contemplation of Hill's masculine miniatures remind us of the biographies and histories of English literature, the functionalism of American Puritan life, the writers of the Colonies, and again, those American writers of the Civil War era?

Why, as we view Hills' regionally inspired floral pastels, are we reminded of French Impressionism in painting and literature, pausing to be certain, yet linger longer and more comfortably amidst epistemological issues in the prose of Bishop George Berkeley; the poetry and prose of New England's Transcendentalists; or even Hills' own contemporary, Sarah Orne Jewett, (author of *The Country of the Pointed Furs*), the Local Colorist from Maine who purchased Hills' first-offered saleable work? Why are we reminded of the long tradition of journalistic recorders of American naturalism, such as William Bartram (*A Drawing of the Round-Leafed Nymphia as Flowering*) and the celebratory writings of Walt Whitman (*Leaves of Grass*) which celebrate as remarkable even the most minute species of the nation's botanical and animalistic creations?

If, as the knowledgeable art critics of the early twentieth century position our curious intellects in the direction of France, especially in the development and analysis of light; why then, inexplicably yet intuitively, do we feel more comfortable grappling for explanations of Hills' art amidst prior centuries of historical development in the art and literature of America and New England? To American art history, of what significance is Hills' unique *oeuvre*? What is Hills' relationship to the aforementioned factors and the concomitant influences of Naturalism, Impressionism, and Regionalism? These are the questions this book attempts to answer as Hills transforms everyday, ordinary objects into symbolic icons heralding the advance of an entirely new aesthetic style - her regional, romantic, aesthetic Lyricism - leaving us to ponder the *oeuvre* of America's Lyrical Impressionist - Miss Laura Coombs Hills.

Diane Elizabeth Kelleher
Shrewsbury, Massachusetts
Manuscript written 1979, edited 2020.

Laura Coombs Hills Chronology

September 7, 1859 -

Laura Coombs Hills is born to Philip Knapp Hills and his wife, Mary P. Gerrish Hills, in Newburyport, Massachusetts.

General early education acquired at Newburyport, in the public school system, and with Miss Emily Andrews.

Studied art with Helen Mary Knowlton, William Morris Hunt's most important student and at the Cowles Art School

1880s -

Painted landscapes displaying Barbizon School influence.

1882 -

Mature art education acquired in New York at the Art Students' League; and as a pupil of William Merritt Chase.

1889 -

Exhibition at J. Eastman Chase Gallery in Boston including pastel landscapes, portraits and flowers titled "The Marshes Near Newburyport" "Aunt's Garden" and "Old Fashioned Flowers".

Illustrated children's book titled *The Birds' Christmas Carol* by Kate Douglas Wiggin.

Prior to 1890 -

Early professional positions included teaching assignments in Cleveland, and later, Boston.

Decorative Arts Designer for the Merrimac Potters, Massachusetts.

Sold illustrations to *St. Nicholas* childrens' magazine.

Decorative Artist for Louis Prang Chromolithographers in Boston where she designed artwork for calendars, Valentine's day cards, needlepoint, cross-stitch and embroidery patterns.

Hills' design work displayed a "strong kinship with Art Nouveau".

Published first professionally recognized artwork: *Flower Folk* by Anne M. Pratt, with Laura Coombs Hills as illustrator.

1890-1899 -

Unknown date. First public review of theatrical talents including: design, direction, and choreography for the Boston Museum of Art's Annual Artist Festival; later repeated for the "Pageant of the Year" held at Mechanics' Hall.

1890 -

Traveled to England with brother, Oliver, and friend, Beatrice Herford. Hills' first exposure to miniature painting on ivory occurred on this trip.

Between 1890 and 1929, Hills made five trips to Europe.

Exhibited with The Boston Water Color Club at the Fourth Annual Exhibition at J. Eastman Chase Gallery.

1892 -

Acquisition of the first two significant art memberships: The Copley Society and The Boston Water Color Club.

1893 - (Also listed in other sources as 1895) -

"Seven Pretty Girls at Newburyport", Hills' first exhibition of miniature portraits on ivory, held at J. Eastman Chase gallery in Boston. First patron was authoress Sarah Orne Jewett. The girls were Annie Brown, Alice Creasy, Mary Huse, Georgiana Perkins, Harriet Perkins, Ethel Reed and Elizabeth Richardson.

1895 -

Received first medal; awarded by Art Interchange for best miniature in a selection during a New York exhibition.

1896 -

Painted a memorial portrait of the late Emily Dickenson from a photograph provided by her sister, Lavinia, which appeared between 1913 and 1937 in books on Emily written by her niece Martha Dickenson Bianchi.

1897 -

First miniature painter elected to the Society of American Artists.
Dream Roses, a calendar featuring young women surrounded by flowers displays the influence of Art Nouveau.
Art Amateur Silver Medal for Best Miniature of a collection awarded.

1898 - (Also listed in other sources as 1899) –

Helped found the American Society of Miniature Painters. Elected first vice president.

1899 -

First exhibition of flowers in pastel, held at J. Eastman Chase gallery; initiating an annual tradition Hills would honor until the year of her death.
First important out-of-town exhibition of miniatures in Paris.

1900 -

Exhibits at Paris Exposition. Receives Bronze Medal.
Establishes Beacon Hill studio in Boston.

1901 - (Also listed by Child's Gallery as 1900) -

Awarded a bronze medal at the Pan American Exposition.
Awarded a silver medal at the Buffalo Exposition of 1901.

1902 -

Charleston Exposition judges award Hills a silver medal.
Receives Second Prize, Corcoran Art Gallery, Washington D.C. for "Fire Opal" miniature.

1903 -

Hills is listed as Vice President of the American Society of Miniature Painters.

1904 -

Universal Exposition judges in St. Louis award Hills a gold medal.

1905 -

Hills designs and has built "The Goldfish" - her home in Newburyport.

1906 -

Elected Associate Member of the National Academy of Design.

1908 -

Hills purchases "Patricia" her beloved antique doll from a London shop.

1914 -

Participates in the First General Exhibit of the newly formed Guild of Boston Artists.

Early in the summer, Hills sends miniatures to London, England, for the show of "American Society of Miniature Painters in London, held under the auspices of the Royal Society of Miniature Painters."

Designs costumes for "Every Boy" to be staged at the Bijoux Theatre.

1915 -

Awarded the Medal of Honor by judges at the Panama Pacific Internacionale Expocicion.

Travels *alone* to San Francisco and then on to Oregon and Washington.

1916 -

Awarded the Miniature Painter's Medal of Honor (Bronze) and Life Membership in the Pennsylvania Society of Miniature Painters.

1917-1919 -

Exhibited with "The Group", a group of women artists headed by Lucy Scarborough Conant.

1920 -

Wins the Lea Prize of $100.00 and the Lea Medal from the Pennsylvania Academy of Fine Art, awarded for accuracy, precision in delineation, proportion, detail, and simplicity of her miniature.

1922-1923 -

Travels to Europe.

1926 -

Boston Museum of Fine Art buys "Larkspur, Peonies and Canterbury Bells" (E. K. Gardner Fund).
Exhibition of Pastels and Flowers at The Copley Gallery, November 22 - December 11.

1927 -

Boston Museum of Fine Arts' C. H. Hayden Fund buys "The Nymph".

1928 -

Rosina Cox Boardman establishes the Levantia White Boardman Medal and Prize ($100.00) given to Hills by the American Society of Miniature Painters.

1929-1930 -

Hills travels across Europe. Exhibits pastels at a variety of galleries.
Contributes "Mrs. Roger Warren" to her last miniature exhibition - the Twenty-ninth Annual Miniature Exhibition in Pennsylvania.

1945 -

Retrospective Exhibition of Pastels of Flowers by Laura Coombs Hills.

1949 -

"Patricia", Hills' beloved doll, is placed on display at H.W. Pray's Department Store. Hills' home, "The Goldfish", is sold and Hills moves to Essex Street.

1951 -

Patricia is donated to the Old Newbury Historical Society, Newburyport.

Twenty-four miniatures are offered to the Museum of Fine Arts, Boston. (Other sources posit 15 miniatures offered.)

April 8th Boston Sunday Post article "Flower Artist at 91 Finds Work Still in Demand - - Has Won Many Medals".

February 21, 1952 -

Hills passes away. "Laura Coombs Hills, Noted Artist, Dead at 93" at Newburyport. (United Press article dated February 21, 1952).

Boston Traveller. "Laura Coombs Hills". February 21, 1952.

Her papers are located at the Archives of American Art in the Smithsonian Institution and The Historical Society of Old Newbury in Newburyport, Massachusetts.

2001 -

Retrospective show "A Woman's Perspective: Founding and Early Women Members of the Guild of Boston Artists, 1914-1945" at the Guild of Boston Artists.

During her lifetime, Hills exhibited regularly at Doll and Richards, the Copley Gallery, and the Guild of Boston Artists, the National Academy of Design, the Pennsylvania Society of Miniature Painters and the Boston Society of Arts and Crafts. She was also a member of the Woman's Art Club and an Associate Member of the National Academy of Design.

2009 -

Portraits From My Garden exhibition co-sponsored by Vincent Vallarino Fine Art, New York, New York; Lepore Fine Arts, Newburyport, Massachusetts; and the Cooley Gallery, Old Lyme, Connecticut; November 12, 2009 at the Boston International Fine Art Show; November 21 - January 2, 2010 at the Cooley Gallery.

Section One

Biography - Life in Newburyport

On September 7, 1859,[8] the authors of the Boston Blue Book penned yet another name into the ledger pages of their membership roster as Laura Coombs Hills was born to bank Treasurer and City Alderman, Philip Knapp Hills and his wife, Mary P. Gerrish Hills, in the Atlantic coastal town of Newburyport, Massachusetts. Little is known of Laura's father except that he was active on the School Committee, the City Council, and served as Director of the Newburyport Public Library for thirteen years. Far less exists to be learned of Hills' mother, except perhaps the most important thing, that together with her husband, the couple provided a comfortable home for all of their children including Laura, her two sisters, Lizzie and Mary, and her two brothers, Robert and Philip Knapp, Jr., for all the years of their childhood in the house on the corner of Washington and Market Streets.

Hills' formal art education was preceded by a general education acquired through the Newburyport Public School system, and attendance at the school of Miss Jane Andrews, authoress of several books including: *Seven Little Sisters; Each and All; Ten Boys Who Lived On the Road from Long Ago 'Til Now;* and principal of her own progressive school popular with Newburyport's monetarily well-endowed. Later on, Hills studied with Jane's sister, the artist, Miss Emily Andrews.[9]

As Hills grew up her artistic education became more characteristic of Boston area artists of her own time, during which aspiring artists, both ladies and gentlemen, often attended the Cowles' Art School,[10] or were tutored independently by an older artist, someone such as Helen Mary Knowlton or J. Appleton ("Appleblossom") Brown, who resided nearby in West Newbury, before choosing to attend either the Museum of Fine Arts School in Boston, The Art Students' League in New York, or one of several foreign centers of academic learning then available, such as the *Ecole des Beaux Artes* or the *Academie Julian*. Both European centers were bastions of timely, advanced and classical learning which incorporated into the curriculum, aesthetic directions derivative of Neoclassicism, Romanticism, Realism, and later Impressionism. This was a fertive, learned, exciting time in the Arts. This was, after all, a century of developments in Modernism and active Academic legacies as well, which looked back to the aesthetic criticism of Maurice Denis and Emile Zola in France; James Jackson Jarves and Henry Tuckerman, both writing in the shadow of John Ruskin in America; and the Modernist critics Sadakichi Hartmann, Clement Greenburg, Frank Mather, Royal Cortissoz, and William Huntington Wright.

There was, of course, the opportunity to study outside America and France; in England, Italy, or Germany; but Hills decided upon an indigenous education at the Art Students' League in New York, where it so happened, that an interesting painter was busily at work. This painter was William Merritt Chase. The work which so whole-heartedly engaged him, beyond his own painting, was the process of educating students: a process effected prior to solidifying his Boston connections, but one equally significant for its effect on his protégés: two in particular with surnames of Knowlton and Hills. All together, factual analysis of the periodical literature of her own time leads us to conclude that Hills' artistic education was surprisingly minimal, even more so, when compared to both the professional status she achieved and to her importance as a conduit of culture in America. Hills' entire education consisted of: study with Helen Mary Knowlton "during three winters"; "three months in New York at the Art Students' League"; and of course, time invested at the Cowles Art School; and the youthful *essays* and *etudes* conducted under the guidance of Miss Jane Andrews.

Despite her training, the true directions of Hills' art, indeed its very origins were twice informed and altered by happenstance. During her formal schooling neither pastels nor miniatures preoccupied her time. While Hills' formal attempts were presaged by a more telling general and spontaneous interest in artistic creations as she casually and fortuitously arranged and then copied them - her later, more spontaneous attempts soon led to the creations most readily admired and formally accepted by her critics and the public. These were, of course, her late Impressionist floral pastels.

Although accounts of her first gleaning of an interest in art vary: the Boston Sunday Post suggesting that Hills arranged some pussy willows in a kitchen tumbler at which point: "One of mother's friends...said...'Send that girl to Miss Emily Andrews for painting lessons'":[11] while another account by noted American art dealer, Robert Vose, Jr. suggests the inspiration emanated from a bunch of Innocents which Miss Emily Andrews brought to paint in watercolor; the effect of each account is consistent and fortuitous: Hills began her love affair with the artistic rendering of flowers. This latter, much-discussed, youthful work now rests in the capable, curatorial hands of the Newburyport Historical Society, while others of her award winning creations remain among the holdings of museums and Boston area estate owners. Later, as we will learn, in the case of her work in miniature painting, another chance meeting, this time on English rather than American soil, provided the impetus for a newly launched direction in her career.

After Hills had completed her artistic training, and prior to her 1890 trip abroad, Hills taught art in Cleveland for a year or two, and thereafter in Boston's Studio Building where she also designed cards and calendars. During this time, in the spirit of Victorian eclecticism, Hills experimented with a variety of media. She produced crayon portraits, painted floral designs on china (for the Merrimack Potters), created embroidery and embroidery designs, cross-stitch patterns, water color landscapes, manuscript illuminations for poems and short stories, designs for Christmas cards and posters,[12] and later, designed an elegant, minutely detailed wardrobe of *haute-couture* fashion for one of her favorite friends - an antique doll named Patricia.[13] Interwoven among all of these accomplishments are the common threads of elegance, color, linearity of design, concern for minutiae, delicacy of scale, and a feeling of broadly defined decorativeness: all stylistic qualities helpful to her work as a pastelist and prerequisite for her success as a miniaturist.

Hills also became involved in stage production in Boston. The May issue of "Time and the Hour", a periodical popular in 1890, mentions that:

> Upon the world at large here in Boston, Miss Hills sprang...as 'the Snake' of the first Artists' Festival at the Art Museum (Boston). Mr. Gaugengigl could not at first be brought to acknowledge the regulation character of the costume of which Miss Hills submitted a sketch, and was only induced to sanction it through the entreaties of many friends.[14]

It was an extraordinary success, and was repeated at the great "Pageant of the Year" which Miss Hills "got up" at the Mechanics Hall two years afterwards - "a most remarkable production altogether." As we learn from another period publication, Hills' involvement with the stage progressed to an organizational level among the hierarchy, such that she now assumed responsibility for origination, supervision, choreography, and costume design, in addition to her amusing role as a performer (the Snake) in December's annual production of the Pageant of the Year at Mechanics Hall.[15]

While critics have heralded John Singer Sargent's influence on Hills' miniatures, the influence of the lessons learned in the realm of theatre, of significant import, have gone unnoticed. While there are numerous artistic sources and influences at work in the development of Hills' artistic style, relative to her miniatures, that theatrics have a distinct impact is readily apparent in the simplified, bold drama of miniatures as diverse as: "The Butterfly Girl", "Daffodils", "Miss Ruth Graves", and "The Yellow Scarf". Here, drapery swirls as if the era's poetic metaphor: some surrogate of emotional tension, a tempest controlled, tersely played off against a cool demeanor, the contemplative faces of inamorati demurely posed, each with her best side to the audience. The chairs themselves, where they exist at all, look less like well-manicured antiques and more like stage props, like secondary spatial foils used to accentuate the more important faces, fabrics, and figures of their occupants. In addition, Hills uses contrasts of local color in broad, bold, sweeping areas, paired down to the bare essentials of modeling, highly characteristic of stage sets in which simplified designs visible at a distance, put forth the essentials of space and physicality and, overall tone and emotionality.

While the exact dates of Hills' tenure are difficult to ascertain, it is clear that her first noteworthy commercial employment in private industry, rather than in teaching, was associated with Louis Prang Chromolithographers in Boston[16] sometime during or prior to 1888, thus several years after completion of her art school training, yet prior to her European travels.[17] Two of Hills' valentines, copyrighted by Prang and reproduced in *The Chromolithographs of Louis Prang*, are still available for viewing today at the Boston Public Library.[18] That Hills chose employment amidst an industry in which the elements of line and color were especially important, amidst a type of graphic medium with concerns similar to etching and engraving, themselves particularly amenable to past American Colonial precedents and certainly mezzotints of a contemporary time in English art, is interesting to us as it not only foreshadows directions assumed later in her *oeuvre*, but provides another of the many important interrelated variables in the historical depository of cultural linkages: artistic, literary and philosophical, binding American and English cultures, as reflected in the *oeuvre* of Laura Coombs Hills.

We may also note that valentines, like flowers, assumed a romantic importance among friends and lovers rarely approached in the faster-paced, less sentimentalized modernity characteristic of our own decade, since they evoked an all important Victorian preoccupation with the expressive languages of love, dialects clearly comprehensible to English and American painters and poets throughout the centuries. No less contributory to the American culture of romance were images produced by the miniaturists of the American Civil War era - and Hills' own beautiful creations.

For Hills, romance may have been elusive in her personal life, but was nonetheless significant in her work, as Hills establishes there, for Romance, an identity and aura all its own and highly contributory to the success of her professional life.

In 1890, Hills embarked upon an important social trip to England, with Beatrice Herford (the monologist) and her brother, Oliver.[19] As the now twice told tale is recounted yet again, Hills:

> ...had been in England on a visit and a young English girl, seeing some of her work had asked her why she did not paint miniatures. Her reply was that she did not think she would like to. But under persuasion she had purchased some little pieces of ivory and brought them home with her intending to make experiments. Up to that time she had done some illustrating and decorative painting, work on China and in commercial design, good work, but not of a kind supposedly advancing. Back in Newburyport, her home, Miss Hills set to work, secured some young girls to sit for her and employed her medium as best she could...
>
> The result was amazing. In a very short time seven miniatures were completed and a new vital personality in the world of art discovered. For from the moment Miss Hills took up miniature painting, she stood, not only alone, but in the forefront of those in this field of endeavor, coming as it were, full-fledged into her own. ...She had no traditions, she had not studied the miniatures of the earlier masters. She selected her own road and followed it fearlessly. Her expression was perfectly natural and at the same time simple, and although it has since been improved and refined, it is today much as it was then, broad, frank, and very individual. Obviously, Miss Hills had genius, that inborn gift without which no amount of training can really avail.[20]

That Hills' most significant encounter with miniatures occurred in England was not coincidental, but rather, predictable. It was equally: predicated on tradition; decisive for the direction Hills' career would assume; predictive of important influences affecting an alternative view of American Impressionist offerings, as predicated not on the art of France, but of England; generally reflective of the overt and covert influence of English art and thought on American culture; and hence, contributory to new directions in nineteenth and twentieth century art in America. The concept of tradition, varyingly assumed as it is absorbed through different cultural agents of Europe and America, affects Hills' art in numerous coincidental ways: coincidental, that is, only initially and apparently, and only until we explore the common underpinnings of these various traditions. It is then, after the aesthetic fog dissipates, that we are treated to insights and revelations into Hills' work which are afforded by analysis with such sources as literary traditions, both American and English, as they respond to societal change; the competitive Anglo-Saxon hierarchical relationships; American artistic traditions including those particularly influenced by English sources and the French artistic heritage as its contributions are mitigated through English contacts.

Yet, curiously, if it were not for a tradition of another sort, a then recent import of German derivation, Hills may not have made her all important trip to England at all. By the 1880s, two important traditions of German extraction were in the process of popularization and assimilation within the mainstream of the cultural psyche of Victorian America: Kindergarten and vacations. With the growing acceptance of the latter, the American professional classes followed in the footsteps of America's more leisurely class, in their well-ensconced tradition of European travel; if however, accomplished at a fraction of the cost in terms of time, money, and requisite auxiliary staff. Clearly, America's wealthier classes were already in possession of well-established leisure-time patterns, including time spent at national vacation haunts such as the horse trials of Sarasota Springs or the coastal and religious retreats which had sprung up as resorts at the ends of the railroads,[21] in fact, financed expressly by the railroads for such a free-spending crowd. There were also steam-liners ferrying guests and freighting cargo: many guests, many trunks, all full of everything from bed linen and towels to evening gowns and full, dinner dress. Many necessities were mandated for seasoned travelers who had prepared themselves to spend a month, three months, even upwards of a full year in Europe on holiday. Entrepreneurial resort brochures were not the only literary enticements beckoning Americans to Europe, for just as Colonial explorer-naturalists had once sung the praises of America to the English and other Europeans, now the topic of interchanging populations and their habits provided ample fodder as well, for novelists here and abroad, such as Henry James, as trends reversed themselves and Americans increasingly now returned to their Motherland of Colonial times. Hills' trip, therefore, could hardly be considered as breaking with convention, but rather as coinciding with it: the tradition, that is, of the long-term vacation. Hills' trips lasted approximately one year. In fact, European tours were now not only the prerogative of professional classes, but exactly the thing to be done in order to maintain one's position in proper society. Indeed, as an artist and well-heeled New Englander, Hills was all but obliged to enjoy European holidays and the absorption of culture, as all the while, Hills prepared herself to be a conveyor of culture through the values evoked within her miniatures on ivory and later her floral pastels.

Conceivably, Hills could have encountered miniatures in America, yet this is relatively unlikely, not because there existed no such tradition, there certainly was one, but because during the time of Hills' schooling, America's miniatures lay essentially well-hidden, almost an invisible art form; in contrast to which England's painters on ivory were well-organized and easily discernible. When Hills arrived back in the States, she "returned in September, afire with enthusiasm...(and) she promptly invited the prettiest girls in Newburyport to come and pose for her."[22] Hills' own words are instructive here.

> What a joyous time doing exactly what I wanted to do most. I can remember the studio, the paints, the queer, low light and the beautiful girls whose personalities seemed to suggest different colors. One was so delicate and charming, and for her, I chose a pale lavendar background. Another was vibrant and rosey. Nothing would do for her but a deep pink. And for the girl with the glorious red hair, what but a pale green background?[23]

Here, Hills is speaking of both the subject, the girl with red hair and the finished miniature she referred to as "The Goldfish". The Goldfish would also become the name of her home, a two-story house built to her specifications and so named, symbolically, because the success of this and other miniatures initiated the seemingly unending trend of financial success which was the mechanism of profitability through which she supported herself and her sister, Lizzie, enabling both the enjoyment of their home, their lifestyle, and their contented relationship. The Goldfish miniature was one of seven painted and exhibited at J. Eastman Chase Gallery, Boston, Massachusetts. The show was called "Seven Pretty Girls at Newburyport" and the girls were: Ethel Reed, Georgiana Perkins, Mary Huse, Annie Brown, Elizabeth Richardson, Alice Creasy and the girl whose miniature was nicknamed "The Goldfish".[24] The date of this exhibit varies between 1893 and 1895, with 1893 the more likely of the two dates of show, which was in any event reviewed by Lucia Fairchild Fuller[25], herself a renowned miniaturist, in Scribner's Magazine, not contemporaneously but in a later article in 1920. Hills sold her first work to Sarah Orne Jewett,[26] the author (or authoress, as lady writers were addressed at that time), and Hills received commissions for 27 miniatures as a result of her first public display.[27] Hills was also awarded the Art Interchange Medal for best miniature of a selection in New York for a later showing of these same miniatures.[28] Generally, her miniatures sold for $1,000.00 each.

Although this would be difficult, it would be interesting to verify the exact nature of Hills' relationship with one of her early patrons, Sarah Orne Jewett, because Jewett "the New England Nun", the "Yankee" was a friend of "Annie Fields of Boston in whose famous salon she met Dr. Holmes, Henry James, Phillips Brooks, William Dean Howells, Longfellow, Whittier, Thomas Baily Aldrich"; which places her very much in the center of regionalist and Brahmin trends. "The Hilton's Holiday" is indicative of Jewett's style which strives to reproduce New England's regional traditions and lifestyle, in the manner of a Regionalist, utilizing native dialect in much the same way as Hills' aesthetic regionalism depicts the specific people and flowers of New England.[29] Jewett's personal mantra was *"Ecrive la vie ordinaire come on ecrit l'historie"* which loosely translated means "Write about ordinary life (biography, ordinary events, ordinary objects) as people write about history" - with factual accuracy, dignity, nobility. Jewett's personal paradigm may be taken as representative of Regionalist and American naturalism to which Hills subscribes. Jewett's paradigm merely perpetuates Walt Whitman's ideas and those of John Greenleaf Whittier, William Cullen Bryant, William Wordsworth, which espouse the value of and interest in everyday objects and the ordinary biographical life, including the romantic events of that life as found, for example, in the sentiments of the Civil War miniatures and love letters. The implications of Jewett's advice is the continuation of a common theme in American aesthetic culture: the natural, the ordinary is in itself worthy, and made all the more so, by minor embellishment. This is a notion which coincides with the political concept of democratic idealism underlying Jeffersonian democracy, which is itself perhaps more powerful than art historical sources, as espousal of the ordinary presents numerous opportunities for themes of the ever present conflict between the real and the ideal. Of all American artists active in both media, pastels and miniatures, Hills most succinctly, most successfully reconciles these issues, thus perpetuating perhaps, the unconscious, and economically exploitable, desires of her patrons. This emphasis on the ordinary perpetuates a concept crucial to nineteenth century American aesthetics, and exemplary of one segment of the arts affected by this all-pervasive, essentially political tone. As we delve into literature, philosophy, and painting, we will see how truly important and pervasive are the intertwinings of the real, the ideal, and the abstract. And we will see how Hills' images represent the democratization of Art.

From the beginning, Hills maintained a sitter's book in which she inscribed names and dates by which to recall works she had accomplished, the perusal of which reveals her rate of productivity on an annual basis to range between anywhere from ten to twenty-seven miniatures, generally averaging nineteen or twenty painted ivories in the course of a single year. Hills maintained this pace, painting portraits on ivory until 1930. Her acclaim was widespread and significant, if not internationally, then clearly nationally. But perhaps the most telling critical comment to assess her level of success, and there were many from which to choose, rests within the comment of an art critic who wrote: "To be miniatured by Miss Hills denotes social status."[30] True enough, even if Hills was relatively unconcerned with status, as she once revealed:

> It tired me to be in society. I only wanted to paint, to listen to music and to read.[31]

The artistic organizations with which Hills was most familiar were circumscribed within the boundaries of metropolitan Boston, and most frequently included groups familiar to most of her artistic contemporaries: The Copley Society (originally the student alumni organization of the School of the Museum of Fine Arts); the Boston Water Color Club; Doll and Richards Gallery; J. Eastman Chase Gallery; the Guild of Boston Artists; and the Concord Art Association located just outside of Boston. In addition, as an artist, she was associated with the New York Womens' Art Club; the Society of American Artists; the American Society of Miniature Painters (which she helped found and of which she served as its first vice-president); the Pennsylvania Academy of Fine Arts; New York's National Academy of Design and Knoedler's Gallery. Internationally, Hills was honored by invitations to exhibitions in Paris and the Pan American Exposicion in South America; and an important invitation to exhibit with other miniaturists in England at the Royal Society of Miniature Painters, which was actually the organizational model for its American counterpart of which Hills later became Vice President. After the turn of the century, Boston's cultural organizations, although vastly different from *avantgarde* institutions located in New York, nonetheless remained both healthy and active in their support and espousal of conservative American art, the art of Boston's traditions. Essentially, for Hills, emotionally, aesthetically, stylistically, the Boston area was home.

Yet, Hills' real home was actually not located in Boston proper, as were the various studios she maintained: first, at the Studio Building, later on Mount Vernon Street; 320 Boylston Street; 66 Chestnut Street and later 103 Chestnut Street;[32] but rather in the environs of Boston, in the country setting of the town of Newburyport. It was at "The

Goldfish" that Hills could read novels and other literature by Florence Thompson, Sarah Orne Jewett, Willa Cather, listen to music and accomplish her artwork.[33] Of her in-town studio on Chestnut Street we know only that originally its walls were decorated in a Victorian color scheme of dark green and bright gold, her favorite shades, upon which her flower pastels must have created a striking impression.[34]

In contrast, of her home in Newburyport, we know much more. It had five bedrooms, and began as a model in cardboard made by Hills, who borrowed the design from Beatrice Herford because both women agreed that architectural models were the only way to conceptualize an unbuilt structure, and the best manner in which to afford visualization of airiness, space and a room's ability to accommodate ancestral furniture alongside other homey treasures. Hills made the architectural model exactly to scale, and, apparently, so interesting a phenomenon was this for a woman to engage in at the time, that the event was written about in periodical literature of the era, which describes Hills' home as follows:

> The wide entrance door opens directly into a spacious apartment which serves the threefold purpose of hall, living room and dining room. Broad twin windows, two on either side of the room, permit of plenty of light and air. A fireplace has a central position at one end of the room, its mantel bearing some fine pieces of old pewter. On either side of the fireplace are built in cupboards with upper door panels of glass. The living room end of the room is furnished in raffia and old mahogany; the dining room part entirely in old mahogany. The rooms, in the old Colonial manner, are arranged to surround a central chimney.[35]

Further, excerpts from an article appearing in "The Craftsman" magazine entitled "The House That Has the Quality of An Old Homestead: Built by Laura Coombs Hills at Newburyport", dated 1908, help us conceptualize that which Hills visualized. Perhaps more importantly, Hills' home, like her art, reinforces themes of New England nature and the American past.

> ...(the) house is comparatively new, but so thoroughly does it belong to the atmosphere of this delightful old town that it gives the impression of having been built two or three generations ago, when life was a more peaceful affair than it is now and when a house like this was meant to serve as the homestead from generation to generation...(Hills) chose as

the site for her home a low hill on the outskirts of town overlooking a wide landscape that is typical of New England...(the) grass is not a lawn but grass. The foundation of the building is sunk so low that the grass blades touch the shingles of the side walls...(1) winding gravel path leads to a single step from which one reaches the front porch, and on the sides of the hill, at sufficient distance from the house to give plenty of air and sunlight, are scattered clumps of slim young trees to relieve the wide outlook without interfering with it...(hers) is a house planned on simple lines...(there has been) no effort to adhere to the Colonial style, yet the seeming (overall effect) of the house is the same as the finest of Colonial dwellings. Its shingled walls are stained in a soft light tone of greenish grey, (while) the window frames and pillars are pale buff...(while) a color accent is given by green blinds, without which no New England house seems really to belong in its environment. Vines clamor here and there around the pillars and over the lattice and beside the house a row of tall hollyhocks carry color and life up against the soft grey walls...(The) roof is a low pitched (one) while the grouping of windows is such as to divide wall space in a way that relieves the effect of bareness which might otherwise accentuate a little too much of the severity of the plan. (A) wide veranda runs across the front of the house, is recessed under one corner where the entrance door stands (as a) wide Dutch door that conveys a sense of welcome goes directly to a large dining room with a fireplace at one end and wide glass doors in front (of) which open upon the veranda giving a view of landscape and western sky, (perpetuating) the idea of nearness to nature. Hills departed from orthodox architectur(al practice by) experiment(ing) with a model, planning details of construction and furnishing rooms (on her own, utilizing her collection of) mahogany furniture, (so that) every space was planned. Between the glass doors and the corner there was space for her own desk and a bracket light, shelves for her favorite books (well) within reach...(The) bedroom, upstairs, had just enough room for a four-poster bed...every space was planned with an eye to the best disposition of the beautiful old furniture which forms such a valued part of Miss Hills' possessions. (The) use to which the veranda is put is modern, like an outdoor living room, furnished with a swinging couch and comfortable deck chairs; in warm weather much of her time is spent here. (The) living room is full of convenient nooks and corners, (while) the staircase is the main structural feature in one corner, this end used for a dining room and the round mahogany table with rush-seated chairs forms one of the most decorative features of the place...(a) swing(ing) door leads to the kitchen, directly in back of the dining table...Two tall cupboards flank the fireplace, both practical and decorative, the lower part of the cupboards are paneled, the top part fitted with small panes of glass showing quaint old china inside.

In the right-hand cupboard only the upper door opens, the bottom part of the wall (is fixed), the reason for this is in the kitchen where space is used for a closet for pots and pans and the upper part for spoons and shallow muffin pans. (The) kitchen (could only have been) designed by a woman and a housekeeper, every inch is utilized. One whole wall is occupied by a (type of) dresser she devised, both beautiful and convenient. (A) lower door swings out (for use of) a flour barrel, a rolling board that pulls out, economical use of drawers, lockers, shelf and cupboard room provides ample space for the storage of provisions and cooking utensils...(A) range is placed against the chimney, crick, that covers the white wall space from floor to ceiling and from door to door...(while a) shelf of books offers an opportunity to use time profitably. (The) adjoining kitchen porch makes for a pleasant sitting room, with lattice and built in seats, out of reach of the piazza (generally) an arrangement for (the) greatest consideration of comfort, convenience and privacy of the woman upon whose shoulders the main burden of housework rests.[36]

What unfortunately does not follow by way of description, but that which we know to be true, is that Hills had her own flower garden, lovingly tended by her sister, Lizzie. Lizzie's relationship with Laura may be best described as highly complementary. Through her artistic talent, Laura provided the financial means necessary to support her sister; while Lizzie, by relieving the artist of the mundane, often troublesome responsibilities of domestic duties,[37] home management and supervision of workmen as necessary, liberated Laura from distractions which preyed upon valuable time and concentration, thereby increasing potential and real productivity. The daughters of Philip Hills traveled together, entertained friends together and jointly maintained a healthy social schedule when household responsibilities were completed.

Hills' social circle most often included her friend, Karoline* Burnhome (Bernheimer) of Newburport with whom she arranged several benefits for the French wounded of World War I; Beatrice Herford (Hayward) of Wayland, the owner of a boutique and small theatre (possibly the Volks' Theatre) where Beatrice and Ethyl Barrymore performed; Mildred Howells, with whom she corresponded; her brother, Oliver; and the personages comprising her "Mutual Admiration Society", which included Hills' cook, Jennie Gourley and her housekeepers, Clara O'Brien, Mrs. Little, and Mrs. Daisy Brown.[38]

Of Hills' travels at least six are discernable, and in all probability, there were more than that number. Beatrice Herford, Lizzie and Oliver accompanied Hills to London in 1890.[39] In 1915, she traveled to San Francisco, presumably and surprisingly alone, to personally accept a medal awarded her, then proceeded on to Oregon and Washington. Her European sojourns included one in 1922-23, one in 1929-30, several during the 1890s with Karoline Burnhome; in addition to which France and Italy also found themselves on her busy itinerary.[40] The implications from periodical literature are that her European tours were in the spirit of the extended year-long variety popular at the time. Since her brother, Philip, was for years editor of the Paris edition of the Herald Tribune, her trip to France may have been spurred by a desire to visit her brother. Hers was, after all, "a very closely knit and affectionate family, judging by the many letters Laura and Lizzie wrote home from their lengthy European trips."[41]

Traveling was naturally a source of pleasure for both the Hills sisters, but so too was returning home. Shortly after the completion of her home, The Goldfish, Hills, a frequent recipient of awards for her artistic endeavors, learned of perhaps the most important recognition of her career. In 1906, she was elected an Associate Member of the National Academy of Design.[42] Membership in this New York institution identified Hills as a nationally recognized artist working in the conservative mode of American Academicism at a time when New York Realists were advocating American Realism. In addition, Hills' reputation was now substantially enhanced, as were her financial opportunities, since this group represented one of the country's most significant art markets, the conservative one. This was only one of the many forms of recognition Hills received and only one of several organizations for professional advancement to which Hills belonged. Some of her other more important awards included: the Art Interchange medal for best miniature in a New York selection (1895); the Art Amateur Silver Medal for Best Miniature of a collection (1897); Bronze Medal, Paris Exposition (1900); Second Prize, Corcoran Gallery, Washington, D.C. for her miniature "Fire Opal"; Medal, Pan American Exposition (1902); Gold Medal, St. Louis Exposition

(1904); Medal of Honor, Panama Pacific International Exposition, San Francisco (1915); Medal of Honor and Life Membership, Pennsylvania Society of Miniature Painters (1916); Lea Prize ($100.00) from the Pennsylvania Society of Miniature Painters (1920) offered in conjunction with the Lea Medal; Levantia White Boardman Medal and prize ($100.00), American Society of Miniature Painters; and she was one of four judges for miniatures on the National Jury convened in the United States.[43]

Of her most active memberships, the following organizations stand out: the Boston Water Color Club, the Copley Society (originally the student/alumna association of the Boston Museum of Fine Arts school), the American Federation of the Arts, the American Society of Miniature Painters (vice-president), the Concord Art Association, Corcoran Art Gallery, J. Eastman Chase Gallery, Doll and Richards, Ferargil Gallery, the Guild of Boston Artists, the Society of American Artists, the National Academy of Design in New York, the Pennsylvania Society of Miniature Painters associated with the Pennsylvania Academy of Fine Arts, Vose Gallery in Boston, the Society of Arts and Crafts (designer), and, of course, she was associated with Louis Prang's Chromolithographers as an employee whose work appeared in their auction catalogue. While these organizations represent professional organizations interested in Hills' art; Hills was known to collect the art of Mildred Howells, Oliver Herford and Ethel Reed.[44]

From the Boston Sunday Post ("Flower Artist at 91 Finds Work Still in Demand - - Has Won Many Medals", April 8, 1951) we learn not only that Hills was popular and working up until her death at the age of 93, as the following passage indicates; but also the reason she effected a change from miniatures toward pastels of flowers.

> At 91, the red geraniums proved too much of a temptation for Miss Laura! She sat propped up on pillows in the big mahogany four-poster that belonged to her Newburyport ancestors, and her bright eyes darted from the scarlet geraniums in the window box next door to the full-blown rose a friend had just picked from her garden.
>
> Experimentally, she flexed the quiet fingers lying on the white coverlet. Then she made a flash decision. "Nurse!", she called, in a voice imperative for Miss Laura, "take a pair of shears, go next door and snip off those geraniums. I'm going to paint!"[45]

Even at this advanced age:

Famous artist Laura Coombs Hills, whose miniatures and flower pastels are celebrated throughout the world, didn't intend to end her career at 91. Like all Hills' paintings, this, done in the winter of her life, was snapped up immediately by Mrs. Ernest G. Victor of New York, who loaned it to the Guild of Boston Artists on Newbury Street for exhibition recently.[46]

Hills' iconographic shift away from miniatures toward pastels of flowers was equally appropriate to Victorian culture in America, a beautiful change, and a practical transition. In her own words, the artist explained her views to journalist, Eleanor Roberts:

Roberts: Miss Laura did miniatures from 1903 to 1930, then she turned to flower pastels.

Hills: Very refreshing, (she chuckled), I got so tired of noses and mouths and faces. Flowers will do anything for you.[47]

While Roberts dates this change in medium as occurring in 1930,[48] the date is meant as an approximation, since The Copley Gallery lists Hills as an active participant, indeed a sole participant, during an Exhibition of Pastels and Flowers, November 22 - December 11, 1926,[49] hence, four years earlier. Hills' last miniature exhibition was indeed the "Twenty-ninth Annual Miniature Exhibition" in Pennsylvania to which she sent her work, "Mrs. Roger Warren" in 1930; while her earliest documented miniature exhibition actually occurred in the mid- to early 1890s. Hills places this date at 1893 by her own notation in her notebook of sitters and miniatures, while Lucia Fairchild Fuller favors 1893 in her article appearing among period literature; and 1895 is favored by another article, "Seven Pretty Girls at Newburyport". In addition, Hills may have painted rather than utilized pastel to create floral topics in the early to mid-1890s, as there are vague references to that effect among documents at that time. A trip to France in the early 1890s may have contributed to her interest in combining pastels with the subject of flowers since, as we learn from her letters, she obtained her colors, particularly the violets, from France,[50] since they were unavailable elsewhere.

Dear Mildred,

.... A Newburyport friend has just come home from Paris bringing me three dozen new pastels from my old Henri Roche place. He has died, but his elderly daughters are carrying on. There are...violets...I may never use them, but I soon mean to try...

Your most affectionate,

Laura[51]

A final factor contributing to Hills' change in medium may have included her eyesight,[52] as Hills was extremely nearsighted, and miniatures are after all precisely that, miniatures, and hence increasingly difficult to see in the necessary detail as one ages. One thing is clear, however, Hills loved this new art form of flower pastels:

> To say that Miss Laura lived her work 24 hours a day would not be an overstatement...In Laura's own words:..."That's how I acquired insomnia...An idea would come to me in bed and I'd get so excited thinking what bit of brocade, what delicate vase I could use, or how I could best combine colors, that it would be dawn before I had even closed my eyes."[53]

At this late hour, Hills had a favorite friend, an unusual one, who no doubt kept her company without complaint: her friend was an antique doll named Patricia. This doll was a coveted possession of the artist, and yet another opportunity for her to design with Art in mind; and another occasion for writers to discuss Hills' life and work in their art columns. Freida Manion's article, "Artist Exhibits Antique Doll", provides us with one such occasion as we take a glimpse into the whimsical preoccupations of ladies during Hills' time.

Artist Exhibits Antique Doll

> ... A beautiful little lady of rare charm and poise will make her Newburyport debut next week when Laura Coombs Hills, miniature artist and pastel painter of world renown, exhibits Patricia, her beloved antique doll, in the window of the H.W. Pray Company department store.
>
> With her exquisite waxen face and shining brunette hair actually embedded in her scalp, Patricia is the shining reality of a dream-doll Miss Hills longed for when she was a little child.
>
> For 40 years this artist who had experienced fame and adulation from the outstanding success of her great art had carried in her secret

heart the haunting image of just such a doll, glimpsed one memorable afternoon when playing with her little friend, Minnie Boutin. Minnie's wax doll and trunk full of delightful miniature accessories had come from London and, inwardly, tiny Laura vowed that some day SHE would go to London and buy a beautiful wax doll with real hair.

...It was in 1908 when the artist purchased Patricia from a London shop a few hours before time to sail home to America from one of her many European tours.

The fulfillment of her childish dream has brought to Miss Hills such pleasure that this year, during the month of her 90th birthday, she had graciously consented to display the enchanting Patricia where others may enjoy her winsome charm.

When estimating the age of the doll, Miss Hills decided to dress her in the fashion of 1860 because when she was a little girl, dolls were dressed as ladies rather than as babies. The artist planned the clothes in great detail to carry out the height of style of that period.

Shown in Pray's window, Patricia will wear a voluminous pale pink silk dress with its three flounces scalloped and edged with a narrow dark ribbon called "Pompadour", all sewn by hand by Miss Hills.

The materials used to clothe Patricia are exceptionally fine and some were very difficult to obtain. Miss Hills recalls that she was helped in this endeavor by the late Mrs. Burnhome formerly of 63 High Street of this city...Patricia also has dainty underthings edged with real lace as befitted a well-bred lady of her day. An authentic hoop skirt, a petticoat of fine flannel with a scalloped edge, white silk stockings and black satin slippers were all made by the artist herself. Most fascinating of all are the miniature white satin lace trimmed corsets and these will be displayed in a frame beside the handsomely dressed doll, surrounded by other tiny belongings such as her hand-made kid gloves, a dainty parasol and gleaming Lilliputian sewing shears.

Eventually, Miss Hills may present Patricia to the Newburyport Historical Society...The story of Patricia and her "coming out" party in Miss Hills' Boston Studio some 40 years ago has all been recorded by the artist and will be presented in Pray's window with the doll and her accessories. Miss Hills herself has designed the window display which will be carefully executed by Mrs. Mildred Hartson, employed at the department store as head window dresser. Mrs. Hartson, a member of the Newburyport Art Association, is an artist in her own right and has studied window-dressing in New York. The flowers which will be garland reflecting Patricia's delicate, inscrutable charm, are made by Mrs. Isabelle Sayward after consultation with Miss Hills.

Patricia's Newburyport debut is an occasion of great interest to antiquarians and art lovers as well as children, for this valuable doll is owned by one of the great artists of our time. A native Newburyporter, Laura Coombs Hills was born September 7, 1859, the daughter of the late Philip K. and Mary P. Hills.

A pupil of Helen M. Knowlton, Miss Hills also attended Cowles Art School and the Art Students' League of New York. She won international prizes for her work including the Medal Art Interchange, 1895; Paris Exposition, 1900; second prize, Corcoran Art Gallery, Washington 1901; Silver Medal, Buffalo Exposition, 1901; Gold Medal, St. Louis Exposition, 1904; Medal of Honor, Panama Pacific International Exposition, 1915 and the first award Medal of Honor, Pennsylvania Society of Miniature Painters, 1916. She is also a member of the American Society of Miniature Painters, American Society of Painters, and the Boston Artist's Guild Watercolor Club. For years she worked at her studio on 66 Chestnut Street, Boston, and her work is displayed in many museums, of which the most familiar to local art lovers is the Boston Museum of Fine Arts where many of her lovely flower pastels are hung.

Newburyport is grateful to Miss Hills for sharing her wax doll, Patricia, who like her owner, is a great lady of graceful, ageless charm.[54]

We are already familiar with statistics provided by cold hard data such as organizational memberships, awards and educational information; and we will come to understand the nature, implications and importance of her art, by what the critics saw as praiseworthy in Hills' work; but what additional traits may we surmise relative to her personality and persona? From a talk presented by Robert C. Vose, Jr. at the Historical Society of Old Newbury's centennial birthday celebration of the artist, we learn that Hills was:

> ...a round-faced, sturdy, Louisa May Alcott sort of little girl, judging by her picture in an old photograph, taken with her sister Lizzie and her brother, Robert, but she grew up to be handsome, slender and

oval-faced, with piercing dark eyes. In spite of her talent for acting, she developed into a very Proper Bostonian type of individual, so it may be that the most interesting part of her unusual character and rather quiet and conventional life, is how she could have succeeded in making such an extraordinary popular career for herself.

...The Women's Educational and Industrial Union in Boston profited largely from the pageants which, during the 1880s and 1890s she produced for that organization. She also managed similar entertainments in Newburyport. Incidentally, she was an excellent actress herself. And she was becoming known in art circles as "clever" undoubtedly, though not, as yet, "remarkable".

...In spite of this (her hobby - gourmet food) Miss Laura kept her slim, neat figure all her life and Miss Lizzie was never more than "pleasingly plump". They both also enjoyed society, Miss Laura to talk - she was a brilliant conversationalist - - and Miss Lizzie to listen, both often busy with the exquisite embroidery in which they excelled. They loved to entertain and, when a summertime party was held, a huge Japanese replica of a gold fish cavorted in the breeze outside their door, to welcome the guests. Both thoroughly enjoyed travel, shopping, and sight-seeing - - perhaps the art museums appealed more to Miss Laura, but Miss Lizzie could always find plenty to interest her. In many of these pursuits Mrs. Burnhome joined them. Once when, on one of their trips, Mrs. Burnhome was called home by the illness of her daughter, the sisters felt bereft. Not only did they miss her presence, but they were also appalled at having to deal with the intricacies of travel which she had always managed for them such matters as finding guides, making reservations, doing the banking, and investing hotel accommodations. But Miss Lizzie rose to the occasion and, by the time Mrs. Burnhome returned, she had become quite competent in attending to such bothersome details.

The sisters also spent much time at the Burnhome estate in Newburyport, now owned by Mr. Edward Fitzgerald, and Miss Laura arranged several benefits for the French wounded during the first World War, in the Burnhome garden. As I recall them, they were very lively and exciting affairs, with lovely surroundings, beautiful weather, and crowds of most elegantly dressed people. And then there was another event, a play, "The Romancers", given in a natural setting, behind the Burnhome garden. That was, like the play, pure romance, with a fine full moon to add extra glamour. I believe Miss Laura arranged that also - moon and all!...

(The Hills sisters)...still had plenty of friends who kept in touch with them, including two elderly sisters, residents of the floor above theirs. The younger of the two often did errands for the Hills and speaks of Miss Laura reading "voraciously" and always eager to get the newest biographies, art books and English fiction from the library... (A housekeeper of Hills wrote of her).."Like me, she loves music and tomato soup."[55]

In addition to her friends' observations of Hills' enjoyment of reading, we know that she often exchanged books with her friends, especially books by Florence Thompson about whose work she commented to her special friend, Mildred Howells, in 1930:

> Dear Mildred:
>
> Can't you be more interested in romance and food? (Sends some suggestions of appealing food)...If I have a windfall I shall buy all the Florence Thompson books...Looking at all...photographs...memory of the cottage in Kent...Lizzie and I had in '92. Have you a craft shop at your house in Petersborough?
>
> ...Laura...[56]

Hills was historically minded in that she was interested in genealogical information to the extent that she owned and coveted an antique book written in 1632 by one of her ancestors, "Geneological Data Ancestry and Descendents of William Hills".[57] Further, antiquarian interests are revealed by her preoccupation with her doll, Patricia, whose clothes were created after the fashion of dolls of the 1860s,[58] when they were conceived after the fashion of little ladies rather than as the children or babies characteristic of our own time. And, of course, architecturally, the home she designed evoked an earlier time, the Colonial era,[59] while its contents reflected both Colonial and Victorian influences in the overall decorative scheme. The mahogany bed and rattan chairs were especially Victorian;[60] as was the color scheme of Hills' studio downtown, which was dark green and gold, on the walls of which her pastels would have produced a regal impression.[61]

Hills was not only adventurous as she traveled abroad with her friends but also a concerned, sensitive, and sympathetic friend, who enjoyed entertaining at home, as well. After a lull in her personal literary communications, she asked of Mildred: "How can you be so hard-hearted as not to write to me for so long a period of time?"[62]

> Dear Mildred,
> ..."Love Paradise" is now in the hands of a real estate agent and I expect daily to hear it is sold...I will let you know what he offers...You cannot imagine how I sympathize with you as you are disposing of things that are dear to you...I am fortunate in possessing nieces and nephews who will take everything.
>   Your most affectionate,
>   Laura[63]

The letter above also reveals Hills' modesty about her art, as does the letter below:

> Dear Mildred,
> The best news I have to tell you is that...I have offered 15 miniatures to the Boston Museum of Fine Arts and what is more, they have accepted 'em...They are spread out on the bed in the other room and some day soon Nancy Cabot will take them in a suitcase to the museum. Monday I had a grief. I had to say good-bye to "Patricia" for she was taken to the Newburyport Historical Society to spend the rest of her life. I only hope the children in town will go to see her. Perhaps you will someday. These are not easy times for me - but once in a while I have a good night - and I live on.
>   Your most affectionate,
>   Laura[64]

Once again, Hills seems to surprise herself with her artistic success. Similarly, during an interview, at age 91, we find her still modest as she recounted her fortunate success during a Copley Gallery exhibition at which all 41 of her floral pastels were "sold out long before noon", later warning the reporter to whom she spoke: "But don't say that, it sounds downright immodest."[65]

She was also a perfectionist, searching for just the right vase for a floral arrangement; and she had a sensual appreciation for color and its inherent aesthetic beauty, especially the violet tones; the same tones used in the backgrounds of Colonial miniatures, and in works post-dating American Impressionist painters associated with Philadelphia such as Emile Miller, for whom violet was all encompassing and who was a contemporary of Hills.[66]

Although working in a different medium, painting, and embracing different subject matter, here the female form moving within an interior, the Philadelphia artists reflected a curious preoccupation with a current trend toward compositions delineated in monotones of violet with complements of oyster white; in addition to reflecting an Impressionist trend common also to Hills' work, the cult of femininity. No doubt these violet tones were common amidst the wide variety of species of cultivated and wild flowers located right in Hills' own backyard garden, which she so often enjoyed, perhaps even more so since maintenance was left not to her, but to Lizzie's green thumb of experience.

In an era in which most women were at some point in their lives, usually an early one, happily or not, for motives of love or finance, duly betrothed, Hills remained a single lady throughout the entirety of her lifetime. In addition, research reveals not a single tidbit, nary a nibble, nor a hint of any romantic interlude. Yet, Hills was not an unhappy spinster. Rather, she was an echo of the early manifestation of the self-supporting, autonomous, emotionally, self-contained adventurous career woman; someone women both like herself and unlike herself read about in the novels of Henry James (*The Bostonians* or *Portrait of a Lady*). Outside of the realm of literature, most of the women, strong-willed and self-sufficient of necessity, were to be found among writers and artists - and they needn't be drawn from a search of the *avant-garde*. Demographic and educational trends of the 1880s, for example, reveal an upswing in women seeking higher education for the first time; wherein we may read that feminism and wealth may have intermingled as parents underwrote the educations of their sons and now their daughters as well. Indeed, feminism was, after all, alive and well in the philosophical writings and milieu of even earlier times.

Hills, the career woman, appears at an interesting time in American history since she was born and grew up within a generation of the period in which women in myth, literature and reality could be independent only outside of mainstream American society. The Leatherstockings[67] of the West during the mid-nineteenth century are an extreme example of this type of conceptualization of the independent woman in literary personification, while Annie Oakley represented one such woman in actuality. The general exception to this notion was the widow; while the single woman was still derisively portrayed as a luckless spinster until the nineteenth and twentieth century feminist writers of Hills' generation began to gain a larger audience. Hills, the unmarried lady and the successful career woman, broke through the stereotypes.

Eschewing both literary and real world feminine stereotypes, from the most fantastically derisive and bizarre to the nearly natural; whether from Aristotle's *Politics*[68] which discusses educational systems and roles of women, issues which find parallel and antagonistic expression among the concerns of nineteenth century writings of American feminist philosophers;[69] or Ovid's *The Art of Love*[70] which finds its counterpart in the nineteenth century medical manuals written by male doctors of the Victorian era for women for the express purpose of imparting appropriate knowledge so as to facilitate men's pleasures;[71] or the masculine, eccentric Leatherstockings of the American Wild West; independent women like Hills, which feminists were, had become less uncommon by the time Hills had established herself as a successful miniaturist of women and men on ivory; orchestrated changes in the direction of her career; supported her sister; traveled alone; and designed her own home.

Spoken perhaps partly through convenience and convention, Robert Vose, Jr.'s observant analogy comparing Hills as a young girl to a Louisa May Alcott type of girl, may be further specified to mean of Alcott's *Little Women*,[72] not Beth, not Amy, nor May, but Jo March. Tomboyish and independent, Jo was one image of a young woman who departs New England for New York City in pursuit of a new life and a successful career. Many of the issues which concerned feminists in America in the previous century, reappeared as themes embodied by the actions of protagonists in the novels of the late nineteenth and early twentieth century in America and England. Henry James, for example, mirrored this and another trend unique to American literature of this time period: its preoccupation with European travel, in addition to offering for scrutiny his personas of Madame Merle and Isabel Archer poised among the other more traditional feminine types appearing in his *Portrait of a Lady*.[73] And then there was *Innocents Abroad*[74] and the interesting fact that Henry James and John Singer Sargent (to whom Hills' miniatures have been compared) both frequented the artistic colony surrounding Frank Millet's home.[75]

Hills' career and lifestyle were evidence of the era, a new era, one in which life was now changing for women in America, and actually had been for some time. Hills had the weight and wealth of feminist tradition behind her. Although Madame Blanc wrote *The Condition of Women in the United States* in 1905; Emily James wrote *The Lady: Studies of Certain Significant Phases of her History* in 1910; Sigmund Freud had written of the harmful effects of repression; Havelock Ellis of the psychology of sex; and Margaret Sanger, *Woman, the New Race.*

These twentieth century developments followed on the heels of other writers. The previous century, half-way through which Hills was born, had already stirred intellectual rumblings. Issues which haunted the feminist philosophers of the nineteenth century became the novelist's concerns of the late 1890s and the early twentieth century; while perhaps the most inspiring and significant document of all was written even earlier, as far back as the late eighteenth century. In 1792, Mary Wollstonecraft, living in England, wrote her *Vindication of the Rights of Women*. From this feminist treatise, all else could be gleaned and applied and merged with the special interest causes of the American political system of the nineteenth century: issues such as Abolition and Feminism merged; male Negro education and female White education began with the opening doors of Antioch College in 1850 and Oberlin College in 1841. Liberalized divorce laws protecting women, biological freedom through birth control, property rights, amorous free alliance; all presaged suffragism.

The Civil War had given Abolitionists such as Sojourner Truth opportunities to write, speak publicly, organize, politicize and mobilize: lessons valuable to the feminists, as oppression of all kinds, of Negroes, of women, of children, of the unbaptized foreigner, became moral targets for strong-willed women. The Missionary movements of the nineteenth century were often spearheaded by women willing to travel to foreign countries and cultures hoping to advance religion and civilization. By 1910, there were 10,000 women, equally divided between single and married, in 17 mission fields of which 332 were physicians; and many were associated with the founding in 1911 of the Board of Missionary Preparation.[76] Perhaps the bravest of all, however, was Cynthia Farrar, who went to Bombay, India, as Superintendent of Female Schools as early as 1827[77] urging other women to follow suit and seek for themselves, rewarding, monetarily, fruitful careers. Another important feminist was, of course, Elizabeth Cady Stanton, associated with the Women's Rights Committee held in her hometown of Seneca, New York in 1848. In 1853 Lucy Stone and Stanton agreed to gain reform of divorce laws, liberalizing them, along with a commitment to help women win control over their own bodies. In May of 1869, the National Women's Suffrage Association was formed, the American Woman's Suffrage Association, and the Woman's Loyal National League, as well. Eleven years later, the International Council of Women was held and then, of course, there were the Blackwells: Nette Brown Blackwell had been the first woman to be ordained as a minister and later professor of gynecology at Women's Medical College in London, England. Elizabeth Blackwell wrote *Counsel to Parents on the Moral Education of the Children* which appeared in 1883; and Alice Stone Blackwell, Nette's daughter, dawned feminist robes and continued the family tradition.[78]

In reality, Hills fit neatly into this established tradition of strong women, this new and acceptable niche. In fact, like other women artists of her time, such as Georgia O'Keefe and Lilian Westcott Hale, following in the tradition of pastelist Henrietta Johnson, miniaturist Annie Hall and other such independent women, Hills excelled. This role, created originally perhaps of necessity for her own financial support, became a comfortable lifestyle, exemplary even, and perhaps quite willingly assumed even in the light of other alternatives. While male writers like Henry James were breaking new ground in literature, women artists had, along with women physicians and missionaries, become independent within the context of day to day reality. Beyond Hills' place in feminist tradition, further contributory to Hills' acceptance and happiness with her lifestyle, was no doubt the fact that her works brought respectable prices in the marketplace. During one show, for example, she could earn $7,000.[79] - and this at the turn of the century, a time when art instructors and assistant professors (such as Lilian Hale's husband, Philip) might earn $3,000.00 or $4,000.00 for an entire year's labor.[80]

Altogether, Hills' was a life happily, productively lived amidst art, music, books, travel, success, family and friends, until February 7, 1952.[81] On this date, the Boston Blue Book no doubt took note of another addition somewhere in Boston, as on its pages there was simultaneously registered, the passing of one of its own, Miss Laura Coombs Hills.

LAURA C. HILLS

NOTED ARTIST

DEAD AT 93

Newburyport - Laura Coombs Hills, world famed for flowers in pastel and exquisite miniatures, died here yesterday at the age of 93.

From the age of 18 until a few weeks ago, Miss Hills produced works that were eagerly sought the world over.

She painted steadily in her Boston and Newburyport studios, and until recently, she had an annual exhibition in Boston.

Some of her paintings were acquired for permanent exhibition by the Boston Museum of Fine Arts and the Metropolitan Museum of New York.

She won the Bronze Medal of the Paris Exposition, 1900; the Silver Medal of the Pan-American Exposition, Buffalo, 1901; the Gold Medal of the St. Louis Exposition, 1904; the Medal of Honor in France, 1916. Many of the country's leading citizens were painted in her miniatures. Her flower pastels brought from $100 to $1000 each as soon as they were finished.

Funeral services will be held at 2:30 PM tomorrow at St. Paul's Episcopal Church.[82]

To friends and family, Hills' death meant the loss of a loved one. Even though consistent with proper social decorum, Hills always downplayed her aesthetic accomplishments, perhaps because they felt so much more like social play than actual work; Hills was still an important, nationally recognized artist: an accomplished portrait miniaturist and floral pastelist - America's Lyrical Impressionist. With Hills' passing, American history lost, as well, an important role model, for although perhaps too reticent or modest to publicly verbalize her politics; through the aesthetic politics of her art and the nature of the life she chose to arrange for herself, it is clear that Hills, an accomplished exemplar with full membership rights, could be seated quite comfortably at the conference table of feminist ideals.

Section Two

Marvelous Miniatures and The Critics

Marvelous Miniatures

PARALLEL DESTINIES: LITERATURE AND MINIATURES

All truths wait in all things...I hear America singing...The female equally with the male I sing...I am the poet of the woman the same as the poet of the man, and I say it is as great to be a woman as to be a man. And I say there is nothing greater than the mother of men... It is also not inconsistent with the reality of the soul to admit that there is anything in the known universe more divine than men and women...The fruition of beauty is no chance of hit or miss...It is the harmony of things with man...About the proper expression of beauty... there's precision and balance...Most works are most beautiful without ornament...How beautiful is candor![83]

Walt Whitman.

These words were not spoken by Laura Coombs Hills. Rather, they are composite extrapolations penned by Walt Whitman in 1855. These words pulsate with importance to Hills' own aesthetic treatise, an ethos not similarly penned, but instead expressed visually through the media of miniatures and floral pastels. These words were spoken by a fellow American, indeed, by one of the Nation's most respected poets, one revered predominantly because he celebrated not only, and above all else, but so well, this unique corner of the Earth, this land, his land, our land; this special place located in the heart and mind, the manner and the material universe: the world of our America. Hills' aesthetic would come to echo Whitman's celebratory tone and to mirror his iconographical choices.

While Whitman celebrated America in all her variety: the different geographies of each of her states and the changing faces of her people, Hills would choose a more provincial route, concentrating her artistic energy on the people and flora of New England. Whitman *feted* America in all her unique sameness - the sameness of underlying principles - of goodness, vitality, innocence and optimism, democracy, romance, equality between man and man, no less than equality between men and women, and he did so at a particular time. So too would Laura Coombs Hills.

Whitman both wrote and lived during the American Civil War era. He was a nineteenth century man who knew first-hand that not since the American Revolution had men been so deeply touched by such heightened emotion, by such spiritual turmoil - the collective turmoil of a paradoxically unified yet splintering conscience as clarifies values and legitimizes beliefs. Against this harsh and divisive Civil War backdrop, tearing at the heart of his land, at his own heart, he poetically annotated forged principles and captured sensibilities whose grasp, if not conceived in primordial sentiments, cast their reflections well beyond his own lifetime into Victorian America and the twentieth century.

These sentiments were those bound by an appreciation of the innate dignity and value of people, being all the more acutely felt, all the more poignant, for having been framed against a backdrop of loss - potential and actual loss of men, and hence the suffering of their women; the splintering of the bonds of sentiment between brother and sister, husband and wife, mother and son. Yet peculiarly, all was born out of love - love of family, love of country. It was this broadly based love of a People, and of the individualized love of people, which gave rise to the need to remember, to frieze memories. Whitman's ethos, like Hills', would give rise to the tiny individual frieze of recollections vouchsafed on ivory, to the American interest in small, hand-painted, portraits in miniature. Mirroring the same concern for a patron's construction of a legacy, Hills revived the celebratory art form of miniatures.

Through them, equally then as now, the contemplation of these tiny treasures, the miniatures of the Civil War epoch and of Hills' twentieth century era, these cultural symbols, these personifications of personality, these icons of American politics, these novelties of aesthetic expression, continuously effect a recollection of Whitman's celebration of all Americans: "I hear America singing...the female with the male I sing...I am the poet of the woman the same as the man...And I say it is as great to be a woman as to be a man." What greater subject than personhood? What truer subject than the portrait?

While beyond the scope of these writings, it must be noted that the iconography of the portrait has a long history, as does the form of the miniature, and the confluence of both. Cognizant of the era of Victorian Forget-me-not bouquets painted on ivory, America's Lyrical Impressionist, Laura Coombs Hills, would hear with her heart, the lingering spirit of these indigenous choirs of America as she painted on ivory the visages of her own era's visual inspirations.

Whitman had placed his finger on the emotional pulse of a nation, isolating the invariant variable as transcends time: the seemingly capricious and independent emotion upon which all else in life - country, God, nature, family, romance, and we ourselves, for our very existence depend: Love. The bejeweled cameos of portraiture, miniatures, experienced their second coming of age in America during Whitman's Civil War era as the love-lockets of sentimental women. Easily transportable, if not so tiny as to be worn about the neck in the tradition of an amulet, then at least small enough to be held in one's hand - cherished, pondered, coveted in private, safeguarded in secrecy, or even boldly, proudly hung on parlor walls. If for all posterity, Whitman had placed his finger on the country's literary pulse; Hills, the revivalist, would through her exquisite miniatures, paint its visual heartbeat.

While most early American miniatures were painted portraits of men undertaken in the interests of women - a tradition which reached its apex with soldiers' images during Whitman's Civil War era; Hills' later works were mainly of women, presumably for men. If there were sentimental women, were there also sentimental men, for each and all of whom these miniatures were timeless treasures? So suggest the amatory letters of American history for they inform us that expressions of love and longing, alongside miniatures, made a remarkable debut during the Civil War era of Whitman; and no less so during the Victorian era, thus presaging a parade of resurgence, another coming of age for these tiny ivory icons effected during the late Victorian, turn-of-the-century times of Hills. Just as Whitman had accomplished much in the process of poetry; it remained for Hills to exhibit her *forte* in the visual realm, in the sensuous naturalism of her pastels and the personal pensiveness and drama of her portraiture.

If the American Civil War era of Whitman and the portraits of its soldiers helped to bring to the forefront the pre-existing penchant for the quality of "sense" in art - that is, the visual verisimilitude, the physiognomic exactitude, the empiricism of what is actually seen in these portraits of soldier's faces; then Hills' revivalist exemplars speak to that empiricism in the visages of both her ladies and gentlemen in miniature. Hills' portrait renderings, her critics advise us, were remarkably true in depiction of the sitter's actual presence and soul.

An *object d'art*, miniatures are equally Art and hence symbol, object and hence "item", biography and hence portraiture. Miniatures are categorical characterizations of physiognomic verisimilitude and spiritual representations of character - as well as records of individual and common history - manifestations of the spirit of both person and time, spoken in a particular language of style. Thus, we acknowledge that miniature painting in America evolved out of a cultural milieu.

That cultural milieu was one characterized by a civil law society: by materialism, capitalism, ambition, property rights, and individualism. The orientations predisposing its creation, nurturance, and success, derived from reliance upon English philosophy as transmitted across the Atlantic during the initial settlement period, in a process which touted values inherent in Theology, Naturalism, Empiricism and such personal property rights as are associated with this shift from Natural Law Society to a Civil Law Society.

Both Whitman and Hills were artists who were representative of American culture. Both were tradition-bound yet unique. That which differentiates Hills from American traditions, is not that she chose the iconography of portraiture: that is well within the realm of American tradition. The distinguishing element is the type of traditional portraiture that she did *not* paint. Hills did not pictorialize the competitive cataloguing of material wealth of America's civil law society as found its way onto other artists' ivories in the form of immortalized miniature portraits of America's mansions and businesses. Further, Hills did not paint predominantly men, but rather typically painted beautiful women. We note her first exhibition was of "Seven Pretty Girls of Newburyport".

And surely few viewers can contemplate Hills' "The Goldfish" without thinking of the Englishman Edmund Burke's notions of beauty, or such lyric verses of the "Romance Poets"- Lord Byron, Percy Bysshe Shelley, and William Wordsworth - as are presented on the following pages.

LOVE'S PHILOSOPHY

I

The fountains mingle with the river
And the rivers with the Ocean,
The winds of Heaven mix forever
With a sweet emotion
Nothing in the world is single;
All things by a law divine
In one spirit meet and mingle,
Why not I with thine?

II

See the mountains kiss high Heaven
And the waves clasp one another;
No sister-flower would be forgiven
If it disdained its brother;
And the sunlight clasps the earth
And the moonbeams kiss the sea;
What is all this sweet work worth
If thou kiss not me?

Shelley[84]

TO -

I

I fear thy kisses, gentle maiden,
Thou needest not fear mine;
My spirit is too deeply laden
Ever to burden thine.

II

I fear thy mien, thy tones, thy motion;
Thou needest not fear mine;
Innocent is the heart's devotion
With which I worship thine.

Shelley[85]

SHE WALKS IN BEAUTY

She walks in beauty, like the night
Of cloudless climes and starry skies,
And all that's best of dark and bright
Meet in her aspect and her eyes;
Thus mellow'd to that tender light
Which heaven to gaudy day denies.

One shade the more, one ray the less,
Had half impair'd the nameless grace
Which waves in every raven tress
Or softly lightens o'er her face
Where thoughts serenely sweet express
How pure, how dear their dwelling-place.

And on that cheek and o'er that brow
So soft, so calm, yet eloquent,
The smiles that win, the tints that glow
But tell of days in goodness spent, - - -
A mind at peace with all below,
A heart whose love is innocent.

Lord Byron[86]

SHE WAS A PHANTOM OF DELIGHT

She was a phantom of delight
When first she gleam'd upon my sight;
A lovely apparition, sent
To be a moment's ornament;
Her eyes as starts of twilight fair;
Like Twilight's too, her dusky hair;
But all things else about her drawn;
A dancing shape, an image gay,
To haunt, to startle, and waylay.

I saw her upon nearer view,
A spirit, yet a woman too
Her household motions light and free,
And steps of virgin - liberty;
A countenance in which did meet
Sweet records, promises as sweet;
A creature not too bright or good
For human nature's daily food,
For transient sorrows, simple wiles,
Praise, blame, love kisses, tears and smiles.

And now I see with eyes serene
The very pulse of the machine
A being breathing thoughtful breath,
A traveler between life and death,
The reason firm, the temperate will
Endurance, foresight, strength and skill;
A perfect woman, nobly plann'd
To warn, to comfort and command
And yet a Spirit still and bright
With something of angelic light.

William Wordsworth[87]

WHEN WE TWO PARTED

When we two parted
In silence and tears,
Half broken-hearted,
To sever for years,
Pale grew thy cheek and cold
Colder thy kiss;
Truly that hour foretold
Sorrow to this!

The dew of the morning
Sunk chill on my brow;
It felt like the warning
Of what I feel now.
Thy vows are all broken
And light is thy fame;
I hear thy name spoken
And share in its shame.

Thy name thee before me,
A knell to mine ear;
A shudder comes o'er me -
Why wert thou so dear;
They know not I knew thee
Who knew thee too well;
Long, long shall I rue thee
Too deeply to tell.

In secret we met;
In silence I grieve
That thy heart could forget,
Thy spirit deceive.
If I should meet thee
After long years,
How should I greet thee?
With silence and tears.

Lord Byron[88]

THE FAREWELL TO A LADY

When Man, expell'd from Eden's bowers,
A moment linger'd near the gate
Each scene recall'd the vanish'd hours,
And bade him curse his future fate.

But, wandering on the through the distant climes,
He learnt to bear this load of grief;
Just gave a sigh to other times,
And found a busier scene's relief.

Thus, lady! Will it be with me,
And I must view thy charms no more;
For whilst I linger near to thee,
I sigh for all I knew before.

In flight I shall be surely wise,
Escaping from temptation's snare;
I cannot view my paradise
Without a wish to enter there.

Lord Byron[89]

ON PARTING

The kiss, dear maid! thy lip has left
Shall never part from mine,
Till happier hours restore the gift
Untainted back to thine.

Thy parting glance, which fondly beams,
An equal love may see:
The tear that from thine eyelid streams
Can weep no change in me

I ask no pledge to make me blest
In gazing when alone;
Nor one memorial for a breast
Whose thoughts are all thine own

Nor need I write - to tell the tale,
My pen were doubly weak;
Oh! What can idle words avail,
Unless the heart could speak?

By day or night in weal or woe,
That heart no longer free
Must bear the love it cannot show
And silent ache for thee.[90]

Lord Byron

THE LOST MISTRESS

All's over, then; does truth sound bitter
    As one at first believes?
Hark, 'tis the sparrow's good night twitter
    About your cottage eaves!

And the leaf buds on the vine are woolly,
    I noticed that today;
One day more bursts them open fully,
    You know the red turns gray.

Tomorrow we meet the same then, dearest?
    May I take your hand in mine?
Mere friends are we, - well, friends the merest
    Keep much that I resign:

For each glance of the eye so bright and black,
    Though I keep with heart's endeavor, -
Your voice, when you wish the snowdrops back,
    Though it stay in my soul forever!

Yet I will but say what mere friends say,
    Or only a thought stronger;
I will hold your hand but as long as all may,
    Or so very little longer![91]

Robert Browning

As we ponder Hills' miniature portraits, we cannot but marvel at the exceptional beauty of Hills' miniature technique, as equally as we revel in the sheer Burkeian beauty of the women represented. Most of Hills' ladies are such lovely, classic beauties, so fully celebrating the glories of their intrinsic femininity as to cause us to wonder: Could these patrons be the artistic descendents of the quintessential loves of whom the Englishmen Lord Byron, or Shelley or Wordsworth speak? We need only look to these writers' poetry to find the preludes to the love of sensibility and the sensibility of Love which infuses Hills' tiny treasures.

The arts of design are usually considered as
commentators upon history and poetry.

So wrote Horace Walpole in his *Anecdotes of Painting in England*. Beyond the basic assumptions; first, that literary trends parallel evolutionary changes in art history; and secondly, that not France but England remains literary Mother to America; inherent herein resides an underlying question: As the poetic handmaiden to an era, what *other* cultural values and evolutionary trends manifest in English poetry and prose do we find reflected in the miniatures of Laura Coombs Hills?

Hills' miniatures were created at a time in American history characterized by a sense of becoming not being, of emerging concerns in the development of both an American national and an American artistic identity. Her miniatures were created by an artistic mind born into the Victorian era, which gazed back toward the cusp of Whitman's America; whose aesthetic apotheosis would arrive forward-poised, glancing coolly and unreceptively, at the futuristic sparks of contemporaneous developments in Modernism.

Instead, Hills' miniatures would come to reflect an earlier time's notions of not only Sense, but Sensibility, lyricism, and beauty. Hills' miniatures function as American personifications, symbols, of the Englishman Edmund Burke's philosophies as put forth in his seminal publication of 1757, *A Philosophical Inquiry into the Origin of Our Ideas of the Sublime and Beautiful."* His inquiry advanced principles devoted toward the explanation of the ideals of beauty and the difference between contemplative romanticism and sublime romanticism. These are concepts which became so all pervasive in Western culture, that they are relevant even to Hills' creations and those of her era's New England (Boston area) Impressionists.

At risk of oversimplification, understanding the poets and the philosopher Burke allows us to articulate the difference between Romanticism and Romance. Generally, sublime romanticism evokes recall of the goal and effect of sublimity, that is, of the capturing and projecting of tempestuous forces of Nature; but especially those forces which elicit activities and cause events arousing extraordinary feelings of terror and awe.

Believing that poetry originates in "emotion recollected in tranquility", that is, individual feelings recalled amidst beauty and serenity; that particular beauty *opposed* to the Burkeian sublime, Wordsworth expresses the soft sensibility of melodic expression of feelings, as is that Lyricism, whose echoes infuse Hills' miniature "Mrs. Platt", as surely as a stolen glance at "Anemonies, Larkspur and Canterbury Bells" proffers a spirit kindred with Whitman's blades of grass and Wordsworth's visualizations of "Daffodils." All Naturalists, Wordsworth and Whitman, Burke, Byron, Shelley and Hills prized the contemplative beauty of the everyday object wherein might breathe such soothing whispers as emanate like sighs infused by the heartsongs of Romance.

Thus, based upon pleasant associations, contemplative romanticism is opposed to sublimity. Contemplative romanticism embodies sensations related to serenity, sensibility or sentiment, romance, love and beauty; all of which evince that endearing, soft-spoken sweetness engendered by the contemplation of the beauty of Nature and the nature of Beauty. For Hills, that iconography embodied flowers, as the depiction of the elements of the Victorian language of Love appropriate to Hills' time; and, as well, women of loveliness.

Moreover, these two iconographical choices share particular expectations of beauty realized in form, stylistically, and temperamentally, as a concept based on pleasant associations, and hence mirror the complementary side of sublime Romanticism - its counterpart of serene, contemplative Romanticism. But Burke's own words are even more insightful.

> By beauty I mean that quality or those qualities in bodies by which they cause love, or some passion similar to it.
>
> I call beauty a social quality; for where women and men, and not only they, but when other animals give us a sense of joy and pleasure in beholding them...they inspire us with sentiments of tenderness and affection towards their persons; we like to have them near us, and we enter willingly into a kind of relation with them, unless we should have strong reasons to the contrary.[92] [In other words, Beauty precipitates an aesthetic and an emotional reaction in the viewer.]

...beauty is...some quality in bodies acting mechanically upon the human mind by the intervention of the senses...We ought therefore to consider attentively in what manner those sensible qualities are disposed, in such things as by experience we find beautiful, or which excite in us the passion of love...[93]

Such qualities would include: *"diminutive"* size, *"smoothness"*, *"gradual variation"* as exhibited by the dove for...It is smooth and downy; its parts are (to use that expression) melted into one another; you are presented with no sudden protuberance through the whole, and yet the whole is continually changing.

Observe that part of a beautiful woman where she is perhaps the most beautiful, about the neck and breasts; the smoothness; the softness; the easy and insensible swell; the variety of the surface, which is never for the smallest space the same; the deceitful maze through which the unsteady eye slides giddily, without knowing where to fix or whither it is carried. Is not this a demonstration of that change of surface, continual, and yet hardly perceptible at any point, which forms one of the great constituents of beauty?...

...*Delicacy*...The beauty of women is considerably owing to their weakness or delicacy, and is even enhanced by their timidity, a quality of mind analogous to it.

The *colours* of beautiful bodies must not be dusky or muddy, but clean and fair...not of the strongest kind. Those which seem most appropriated to beauty, are the milder of every sort: light greens; soft blues; weak whites; pink reds; and violets...Thirdly, if the colours be strong and vivid, they are always diversified, and the object is never of one strong colour; there are almost always such a number of them, (as in variegated flowers) that the strength and glare of each is considerably abated...*physiognomy* has a considerable share in beauty especially in that of our own species.

...The *manners* give a certain determination to the countenance... capable of joining the effect of certain agreeable qualities of mind to those of the body...the face must be expressive of such gentle and amiable qualities as correspond with the softness, smoothness, and delicacy of the outward form...the eye...has so great a share in the beauty of the animal creation...(and) consists, first in its clearness...like diamonds, clear water, glass...the motion of the eye contributes to its beauty, by continually shifting its direction; but a low and languid motion is more beautiful than a brisk one; the latter is enlivening; the former lovely... Besides all this, the eye affects, as it is expressive of some qualities of mind.

Gracefulness is an idea belonging to posture and motion... roundness, delicacy of attitude and motion. When any body is composed of parts smooth and polished...at the same time affecting some regular shape, I call it elegant...(Beauty) excite(s) love and contemplation:...the head reclines something on one side; the eyelids are more closed than usual, and the eyes roll gently with an inclination to the object; the mouth is a little opened, and the breath is drawn slowly, with now and then a low sigh; the whole body is composed, and the hands fall idly to the sides. All this is accompanied with an inward sense of melting and languor. These appearances are always proportioned to the degree of beauty in the object, and of the sensibility, in the observer...*Smoothness* is a principal cause of pleasure to the touch, taste, smell and hearing... easily constituent of visual beauty...found almost without exception in all bodies that are by general consent held beautiful...smooth bodies cause positive pleasure by relaxation.[94]

It is nearly impossible to ponder Hills' images of femininity without noting her adherence to Burke's ideals of beauty. And this preoccupation was felt in England and America. Within this context it is logical to link Hills' lovely women with the beautiful and the genteel, and with the lyric "poets of Romance" as aspects of the eighteenth, nineteenth, and twentieth centuries' broader preoccupation with Nature and the poets who best espoused that tradition - Byron, Shelley, Wordsworth and their Italian predecessor, Thomas Wyatt. In addition, it is also logical to link Hills' aesthetics to the Victorian writers whose ancestral origins are these same Romantic poets; and finally, the lyrical rhythms of Naturalism as are found among American artists enamored with the gentle side, the contemplative side, of Nature. And in Hills' era, this would include the traditional, conservative legacy of the "gentle generation" of artists of the twentieth century, as were those practitioners enmeshed in the Boston culture of Hills' New England such as Hills' contemporary, Lilian Westcott Hale, and even Hills herself.

Thus, we note, as America's cultural identity congealed as increasingly *politically* independent from English roots; after the spirit of Byron, the dominant literary trends still rested upon the lyric shoulders of the "Romance Poets" in their concentration on feelings, human relationships and lovelorn longings for beautiful Nature and graceful feminine beauties. The gentle side of Nature was indeed inescapable as on the American home-front lyric novelists such as Katherine Porter, Willa Cather, and Sarah Orne Jewett penned prose enjoyed by Hills herself.

These artists were, all the while, glancing at Nature through the eyes of the Regionalist ready to glorify a specific segment of the country, and the lyric Romanticist, singing the sweet serenades of the "Romance Poet." This phenomena occurred as an aesthetic response to the stimulus of chaos engendered by the Industrial Revolution. A sense of peaceful respite was the sought after prize artists coveted and attained by choosing to eschew traditional religions and standard social institutions by turning instead toward the emerging new religions: the "Cult of Nature", the burgeoning "Cult of Solitude" and the "Cult of Beauty" - all handmaidens of romantic, contemplative lyricism. And the sense of peace captured in Hills' work was undoubtedly a factor in their popularity with her nostalgic patrons.

Lyricism emerged more significantly, if more eloquently, as an English phenomenon, and clearly so if we recall not merely the love sonnets of Byron, but their dependence upon the stylistic precedence of the sixteenth century, Lyric poet, Thomas Wyatt. For it was Wyatt, who during his translations of Italian forms, formalized and codified poetic lyricism as based on such particular themes of romance as: the poet's disillusionment, the death of the lover, the elusiveness of sleep, the sadness of departure, all presented in a light, melodic manner amenable to being set to music; which being applied to serious content created a particular type of well-balanced tension.[95] Indeed, few may gaze upon Hills' *inamorata* without thinking as the American, Whitman, and the Englishman, Byron, must have done when gazing upon beautiful women, of the themes of romance which so enveloped their forbearer, Wyatt.

Paired with various English and American renditions of Wyatt's themes, Hills' miniatures of women become quintessential exemplars of lyricism; ladies whose demeanor hints strongly at the influence of this trans-generational transmission of notions of British literature upon American thought, literature and art. This is the lyric sentiment which tellingly distinguishes Hills' twentieth century art as oriented toward the nineteenth century; for if her portrait miniatures of ladies are nothing else, they are such ebbing heart-flows of Beauty's sensibilities as smolder quiescent beneath their own guises, transformed into historical, romantic keepsakes as nearly whisper the timeless expression of feelings between men and women.

Lyricism's inherent concepts of sentiment, emotion, romance and individualism are important concepts in nineteenth century American literature, nineteenth century English literature and the twentieth century art of Laura Coombs Hills. Indeed, Hills' miniature of *"Mrs. Charles Platt"* calls to mind concepts of beauty and the essence of being beautiful as we imagine this lady to be far from a solitary creature. Rather, Mrs. Platt is portrayed as a humanly, romantically engaged woman subsumed by sentiment and sensibility, from which arise such common associations with lyricism as represent engagement with life itself. Mrs. Platt seems almost ready to come to life.

Now, the melodic expression of spontaneous feeling, true literary lyricism, partakes of such mechanics of poetry as alliteration, assonance, meter, rhyme and feminine rhyme, thus facilitating that special musical demeanor and delight which may be observed among the previously mentioned poems of the Romance Poets. Thus, artistic lyricism may conceivably be one of style (that is, achieved through rhythmic harmonies of patterning or coloration) or iconography, or both, as is the case with Hills' exquisite matrons and *ingenues*.

Such artistic and literary lyricism appears as a discerning variable, a temporal beacon destined to illume a changing concept of individualism. Nineteenth century America played host to a strong sense of inherited political individualism wherein the sense of self was linked to an earlier legacy of duly internalized, larger cultural norms and legitimized societal institutions poeticized by the sensibility of the century. This was the individualism born of the American assimilation of the ideas of Locke, Hobbes and Dewey - linked to shared values of home, country, honor - and the "good emotions" of Spinoza's[96] citizen in concert with his culture, as bred harmony in a civil society. All was packaged in a Romantic essence. This is individualism freely, proudly intermingling with Naturalism and Lyricism. And it was this psychologically comfortable type of nostalgic individualism which garnered so much appeal for Hills' patrons of portrait miniatures.

However, Hills' twentieth century witnessed the rise of a different type of individualism, with different connotations - an individualism which Hills rejected. For example, Pablo Picasso's *"Desmoiselles d'Avignon"* addressed a twentieth century politic of aggression, alienation, exclusion, and confrontation, quite distinct from the genteel, inclusive sense of warmth and belonging which envelopes and enlivens soldiers' love letters, the miniatures of the Civil War era and Hills' own miniatures.

Iconizing the history of ideas, artists and writers of the twentieth century would increasingly come to reflect introspective propensities, which would culminate in altered form with Sigmund Freud. Individualism may still have been touted as a laudable ideal, but it was not after the towering fashion of politician, soldier or frontiersman. Rather, it was an individualism emerging from the most personal side of the self, often an aberrant side of the self, fixated rather than focused on its own interior life and expression with little reference to legitimized norms. That modernist space and aesthetic systems had begun to fracture, strongly mirrored society: the individual was now a fractionalized version of a once grander, more highly integrated and democratically recognizable self. Sentiment may have come to reign as all important, but it was the sentiment of alienation - of an isolated, drifting and troubled self, like many of Freud's patients. This was far different from the classic, safe, hearth and honor-bound sentiment of individualism so beautifully presented by Hills. Her revivalist miniature portraits, like those of the Civil War era, are images which at least strive to prolong the perhaps mythically nostalgic era of chivalry, honor and dignity. It is little wonder that the critics extolled Laura Coombs Hills as: "One of the country's best miniaturists."[97]

Finally, it may be noted that like many women artists of her own, previous and subsequent generations, Hills art was wholly unconcerned with war and politics. Instead, inherent in her orientation was a deliberate turning away from this side of life, as she consciously embraced the more genteel preoccupations of human nature and earthly life. Her art, her mind, and her heart were pleasantly poised toward a sensitive and sentimental recording of people, and the production in pastel of one of their most delicate and favored amenities - flowers.

The first endeavor, miniature portraits, stems from the earlier tradition of Colonial American art forms which are themselves closely related to a heritage infused with manuscripts and graphic arts such as engraving; and ultimately, the influences of English portraiture. Perhaps even more readily associated with the legacy of miniature artists of the American Civil War period, of Whitman's era, both Hills' miniatures and pastels were curiously accomplished during the end of the Victorian era and the first half of the twentieth century. Thus, in a sense, Hills' perspective is at times - retrospective. At other times, especially in terms of color theory, it is forward-thinking. Moreover, Hills' *oeuvre* combines interests characteristic of Colonial America, Whitman's America, the American Miniaturist Revival of 1890-1930, twentieth century America; and some of the most amenable literary aspects of America's heritage gleaned from England. Hills' aesthetic and her miniatures provide the perfect backdrop for literary expression, both English and American. Hills' aesthetic makes of these forces - parallel destinies.

ESTABLISHED TRADITIONS: AMERICAN MINIATURE PAINTING

As an American miniaturist, Hills is part of an older American tradition. She is both traditional and unique. The evolution of the history of miniature painting in America is essentially one of sporadic development initially emerging from the painterly inclinations of men, beginning in Colonial America and continuing through the Civil War era; then resurfacing once again as a revivalist phenomenon initiated and perpetuated by the artistic endeavors of women. This latter event occurred later in the nineteenth century, as Victorian America prepared to yield its concerns to the embrace of a new century and a very new and different world. Rarely, after this generation of artists active at the turn of the twentieth century, would the technological and mechanistic world of America yield to such clearly nineteenth century preoccupations as these sensuously pleasing, lyrical visualizations of sentiment, beauty and romance - of sense and sensibility.

The first historian of American art, William Dunlap, informs us of eight or so miniaturists of merit during the eighteenth century: John Ramage, James Peale, William Williams, Mather Brown, Thomas Spence Duche, Robert Fulton and Thomas Coran, of whom Ramage is held in highest esteem. Yet, there were still other practitioners including: Otto and Philip Parissiens, Charles Fraser, Rembrandt Peale, Henry Benbridge, Walter Robertson, Andrew Robertson, Edward Miles, Thomas Bishop, William Brich, John Robinson, Edward Savage, John Roberts, Robert Field, Benjamin Trott, E. Tisdale, Alexander Robertson, Edward Green Malbone, Raphael Peale, Joseph Wood, Anson Dickenson, George Munger, Elizabeth Metcalf, Henry Williams, Pierre Henri, Nathaniel Rogers, M. Belzons, and even William Dunlap himself.[98]

As one might expect, there was among these artists an overlapping interest in various other media and even other vocations. Many were first and foremost portrait painters in oil. Indeed, we recognize the name Robert Fulton, the artist, scientist and inventor; and Ramage occasionally painted life-sized images in "pastil" (pastel) or crayon; while Peale painted portraits in oil; Williams used pastels; Duche, oils; and Fulton enjoyed painting landscapes. Dunlap, himself, produced miniatures and portraits and, indeed, with the exception of Robert Fulton (who Dunlap informs us was guilty of painting "poor portraits in Philadelphia"[99]) most of these artists were successful portraitists, if not primarily, then secondarily; since the necessary skills of modeling and modulation (for physiognomy and chiaroscuro) were as equally those

51

of the miniaturists as of the painter. Both have the same desired end: the visualization of verisimilitude in physiognomy and effusions of character.

More similar than dissimilar, the primary underlying thread of commonality binding many of these miniaturists together, transcending stylistic idiosyncrasies, was a shared background in engraving or other graphic activity related to publishing; and hence a respect for draftsmanship representationally appropriated to effectively mirror creations of the natural world. Thus, these artists evidenced a love of empiricism - a love of "sense and the senses". The secondary commonality: iconography, here portraiture, was related not only to American art historical precedent of English derivation, but parallels as well important stages in American literature such as the emergence of biography.

In its turn, nineteenth century America was embellished by the works of miniaturists: Anne Hall of Connecticut, H. Bridgeport, David Dickenson, George Catlin, Charles Cromwell Ingham, William Woolsey, G. W. Newcomb, Thomas Seir Cummings, Henry Colton Shumway, John Wood Dodge, James Edward Freeman, Alfred Agate, Thomas Grimbridge, and George Munger.[100]

Hills' twentieth century, contemporary miniaturists were primarily women and included: Margaret Foote Hawley, Sally Cross, Jean Nuttig Oliver, Alice Beckington, Bertha Coolidge, Evelyn Purdie, Lucy M. Stanton, and Theodora Thayer.[101] In her thesis of 2003, *"Diminished yet Disarming: The Portrait Miniature Revival, 1890-1930,* author and art historian Maryanne Sudnick Gunderson adds numerous insights into the changes occurring during the era in which Hills created her miniatures.

While Hills concurred with the traditional iconography and the traditional miniaturist's background as incorporating the graphic arts; where she differs, where she is unique, where she is innovative is in the area of technical means. Technically, Hills was not the typical miniaturist. William Dunlap's *History* presents us with the earlier, American miniaturist T. S. Cummings' article on the traditional aspects of painting miniatures titled "Practical Directions for Miniature Painting" - watercolor painting on ivory.

PRACTICAL DIRECTIONS FOR MINIATURE PAINTING

By T. S. Cummings, Esq.

MINIATURE painting is governed by the same principle as any other branch of the art, and works in miniature should possess the same beauty of composition, correctness of drawing, breadth of light and shade, brilliancy, truth of colour, and firmness of touch, as works executed on a larger scale...

Miniatures, as they are at present painted are usually executed on ivory, and in transparent (water) colours, and according as the mode of application of the colors to the ivory partakes of the line, the dot or smooth surface, is the style, technically termed hatch, stipple or wash. In the first named, the colour is laid on in lines, crossing each other in various directions, leaving spaces equal to the width of the line between each, and finally producing an evenly-lined surface. The second is similarly commenced, and...is finished by dots placed in the interstices of the lines, until the whole has the appearance of having been stippled from the commencement. The third is an even wash of colour, without partaking of either the line or the dot, and when properly managed should present a uniform, flat tint. Artists may vary in their style of execution...some preferring a broad, others a minute style; though the first is decidedly the most masterly....

The following process I have found to possess many advantages...

Having your colours and ivory prepared, and your subject selected, your next step is to procure a correct outline....Your outline carefully drawn on your ivory, you will next lay in the dark shadows with a light and warm neutral tint, sharp, firm, and of the right shape....you may proceed with the lighter shadows or middle tints...All being justly situated, you then lay in the general colour of the complexion, and having produced the requisite depth, you will, with a sharp lancet, scrape off the shining lights on the face, such as the high light on the forehead, nose, etc...Having gone over all the features, corrected their drawing and colour, you next examine if the drapery and hair of your sitter suit you; if so, copy them...Your picture then is sufficiently advanced to put in your background.

It is commenced with a round-pointed pencil and faint colour, in broad lines, crossing each other at an acute angle, gradually increasing in fineness as you approach the complexion; and then still further finish by stippling...Your background so far advanced, it is time to insert your drapery. If light, you proceed much the same as with the face; if dark, it is treated with opaque colours. The outline previously obtained, you with a full pencil float on a quantity of the colour you wish to produce, always giving it body by the addition of white, and smoothness by laying the picture horizontally during the operation; this will allow the colour to become perfectly flat from its fluidity. When dry, it is ready to receive the lights and shadows, as indicated by your model....Generally you will find the flesh-colour deficient, and the shadows weak; these you strengthen and improve, in accordance with the original, adding such colour as in your judgment you think will render it more like the nature before you; and lastly, give brilliancy and transparency by the addition of gum with your colours, in the dark parts, or wherever else you may deem transparency desirable.

In this we have given direction for the management of a head only; it is however easily adapted to any subject, as the leading principles must of necessity be the same.[102]

While various artists differed in the degree to which each adhered to the principles and proscriptions of miniature art advanced in the aforementioned description, most artists had in common a rather limited choice of iconography. While a demand for naturalistic, landscape miniatures, often combining elements of architecture, scenery, and the human form, in an overall square format, existed; these miniatures were relatively unique, often singular commissions effected by a property-owner desirous of a special artistic record of a home or business establishment. These were icons: tributes to the owner's capitalistic success and strong individualism. Moreover, though, the bulk of miniature activity remained tightly bound to the realm of portraiture; and therein, confined to three or fewer typical formats. Once established, early American miniaturists tended to reflect the portrait style of contemporary painters, and indeed artists often achieved a respectable facility of expression and fluidity of means in both areas and media.

The earliest American miniature portraits were generally simply bust-length renderings of the sitter's head and shoulders. Later, the portrait itself acquired a new standard presentation. The portrait itself was usually positioned slightly off-center rising to a height equivalent to three-quarters of the allotted area, utilizing a three-quarter view with piercing eyes directly engaging the viewer's interest as if by revealing the sitter's soul. In its preliminary stages, artists appeared to have conceived the portrait in a geometric manner, as an oval cranium surmounting a pyramidal torso intersected by the arms, bent at the elbow, situated at perpendicular right angles and echoing first the horizontal and then the vertical lines of what would normally be the ground line and vertical of a canvas. Yet all is neatly and smartly transposed to an oval format reminiscent of a cameo. The backgrounds against which these formally dressed, seriously-minded sitters appeared was stark and unadorned, except for the delineations of shadows caused by hinting at the source of natural light which models the forms and faces of the figure. Clothing was presented as formally elegant, and simply conceived, most often of two tones, one dark and one light, and indeed, it is often that we find miniatures composed of only a basic palette of black and white.

Predictably, alterations to this generally accepted and widely practiced portrait formula occurred. Some noteworthy examples include: the miniatures of Henry Benbridge ("*Elizabeth Ann Timothee - Mrs. John Williamson of Savannah*"); Daniel Dickenson ("*Mrs. Joseph Andres - Sally Solomon*")[103]; later early nineteenth century forms including John Robinson's "*Mrs. Pierre Hurtel*"[104]; Thomas Seir Cummings' eloquently anecdotal miniatures; Nathaniel Rogers' ("*Mrs. Gabriel Marigault*") and Anne Hall's "*Portrait of the Artist with Her Sister, Elizabeth Ward Hall, and Master Henry Hall*"[105].

The manner of T. S. Cummings as reflected by his portrait of fellow painter Thomas Cole and his portrait of his own wife, Jane Cook in "*The Bracelet*"[106] is distinctive; and these works are perhaps two of the most eloquently innovative of all early American miniatures. In the latter work we discover the coyish, anecdotal detail of Jane Cook as she provocatively toys with her bracelet, ever so delicately, ever so coquettishly, while gazing directly into our eyes; perhaps in much the same fetching manner as she attracted the gaze of her husband or perhaps toyed with the hearts of other suitors before her marriage. While the background remains undelineated, one side of the image is given over to a darkly shadowed, Neoclassical urn; clear references, along with the soft texture of the cascading locks of Jane Cook, her creamy skin, and the harmony of sateen lights and textures of the deep folds of her ball gown, to the admiration of formality reminiscent of Neoclassical prototypes; and a romantic prelude to the miniatures produced a century later by Laura Coombs Hills. And here we see a distinction between earlier and later miniatures: the earlier type, like the literature of the time, appeared less factually and anecdotally embellished, much as would the entries in contemporaneous lexicons, or preachments whose English and American mandates had become simplification and austerity. With Cummings, Hall and Fulton we see a change. With Fulton, we have essentially a form analogous to English portrait painting and literary biography, as it introduces historical attributes central to furthering the concept of Ego and his identity.

Later still, with Hall, we have not only the rare group portrait, a composite of ages and relationships; but as with Cummings' *"Jane Cook"*, we discern distinct personalities tied together in a form analogous to genre painting, and the novel or perhaps epic poetry in literature, by virtue of the ever important implication of sequential occurrences in the lifetime of the individual personality. This is most evident in Hall's *"Portrait of the Artist with Her Sister, Elizabeth Ward Hall and Master Henry Hall."* Romantically, sensitively anecdotal details; the inclusion of a still-life composition; decorative floral designs; a compositionally well-planned structure based on the delineation of individual personalities as reflected in Murillo-inspired faces; thus use of frontal, profile, and three-quarter portraits: all combine to yield both an exceptionally enlivened composite of the emotional relationships inherent in the concept of "family" and the actual members of a family. So lifelike in gesture, temperament, and vitality, we cannot help but wonder if Anne Hall's nephew is dreaming the familial artistic dreams of the next generation, as he pensively eyes the peonies and tiger lilies before him, paper and pencil poised, ready to proceed at a moment's notice.

This implied activity, accomplished through gesture, is quite distinct from the interrupted, frozen, candid moments or deliberately arrested poses characteristic of the earliest miniatures such as the heads of *"Thomas Say"* by Joseph Wood, or *"James Stanyarne"* or *"John Deas"* by Pierre Hurtel; all of which form an especially good illustration of this latter, earlier type of miniature since they are essentially merely heads frozen in time, glimpsed for a solitary moment, in the absence of anecdotal detail. The key distinction between earlier and later miniatures is thus that the early ones are simple, staunch characterizations of character and effusions of personality, which yield to the later, anecdotally inspired depictions which hint at lives more fully lived, as the artist exposes glimpses into the personal life behind the characterization.

The softer delineation of fabric, coupled with the lighter backgrounds, and increasingly diffuse textures of the dresses of Aunt and friend, echo a general softening in the portrayal of women's miniatures; and an upcoming trend: As time presses forward, backgrounds become lighter and more diffuse, forcing an increased concentration on the depiction of character, a heightened awareness of individualism mirrored in American philosophy, culture, politics and literature as previously noted.

Children were equally important objects of representation, although they were not depicted within the realm of their own world, replete with tops or other games and miniature furniture; but were instead presented exactly as smallish adults, formally dressed, head and shoulders; their youthful age discernable, not from demeanor, but from facial structure. Later, Hills' miniatures would alter this time-tested formula in favor of young subjects, relaxed, posed and represented in their own children's world.

Generally, as with their adult counterparts of Colonial and current times, even the manner of framing was not left to chance, but rather designed ahead to enhance the manner of presentation of each of these tiny gems. Some miniatures were encircled by continuous beading. Others were bounded by elaborate floral motifs, tiny bits of leaves and nuts, and fruits. All naturally had a significant impact, heightening the romantic overtones imparted to these at times reticent, at times vainglorious, but always grandiloquent *petite tableaux*.

HILLS' ART HISTORICAL STYLE:

If attendance at the local Cowles School, training at the Art Students' League in New York where William Merritt Chase taught, and her encounter with a miniaturist advancing the style of English portrait miniatures were not hints sufficient to elucidate the nature of Hills' painted ivories and their relationship to Boston's special style of Impressionism, then perhaps this was best accomplished by an articulate critic who once referred to Hills as "A veritable John Singer Sargent of miniature painting".[107] Herein did the critic lavish upon her the highest praise advanced in the interests of portraiture, but as well, paired back her stylistic sheathing, eluding to the basis of Hills' aesthetic as a composite of American, English and French influences. Similarly in Sargent we find an American heritage expressed iconographically, intermingled with English underpinnings befitting a resident of that country, and a stylistic ancestry indebted in indeterminate parts to French, American and English Impressionism. And such are the influences as have always enamoured connoisseurs of turn-of-the-century Boston Impressionism, though Hills, additionally, possessed unique qualities derived from solely personal sources.

Like Hale, Hills' stylistic proclivities are aligned with Boston's unique traditions, prevalent among which are: an equal veneration for the principles of draftsmanship, volumetric modeling, and three dimensional perspectival space according to the principles of which objects and figures are correctly positioned commensurate with the optical laws of nature including Renaissance perspective, and local color, all combined with such traditional aspects of design as readily lend themselves to the dictates of verisimilitude and empiricism, intended to advance representations of such subjects as evoked a pleasurable response, presented in a manner reflective of the aesthetic orientations of Edmund Burke, created in an environs conversant with a general respect for principles of art as represented by the vogue for Vermeer permeating the walls of parlor and salon.

> The mechanic arts have accompanied and assisted the fine arts in every step of their progress.[108]

So wrote the nation's renowned, First Historian of American Art, William Dunlap. And, if Whistler's pastels gave rise to the symphony of color harmonies arranged in

58

Symbolist melodies, which Hills may have incorporated as one basis, in addition to English gardening theory and her own horticultural experimentation, for the lyrically inspired complements present in the designs of her floral portraits in colored chalk; then so too, it may be noted that the graphic arts, by definition, in addition to Sargent's proclivities, have influenced her portraits of New Englanders. Indeed, what else, are the majority of miniatures but watercolors, though created not on paper, but on ivory? The graphic arts, and Hills' work, played an important role in the development and perpetuation of Impressionism in New England.

As an artist exhibiting her works alongside such other Bostonians as renowned child portraitist and prestigious Museum School alumna, America's Linear Impressionist, Lilian Westcott Hale,[109] in a city whose elite evermore paid homage to such society renderings as John Singer Sargent's *"The Daughters of Edward Boit"*, (Hale's neighbor and patron); Laura Coombs Hills, America's Lyrical Impressionist, may be considered a stylistic brethren. One common thread interwoven among these artists is the spirit of English Impressionism, that is, of a sort of French Impressionism, whose subjects are more often confined to portraits rather than boulevards and harbors, the colors of whose palettes are inherently refined to sing out in comparatively lowered tones geared to appease the critics and the scrutinizing eyes of the predominantly English patrons as dotted the neighborly maps of demography while inhabiting the stately homes of the city and its environs.

If deviations to this type of Impressionism occurred, they were generally those indicative of the incorporation of the Symbolist's elongated body type, Tonalist color experimentations, the monochromatic moods of earlier Barbizon painters of landscape, the Cult of Japanisme, the occasional foray into Modernist abstraction and the decorativeness of the graphic arts.[110]

Beyond adherence to the tenets of Boston Impressionism, it is perhaps the influence of John Singer Sargent which strikes us as coincidentally, not causally, most significant. Hills never studied with Sargent, yet there is common ground. The critic who termed Hills "a veritable John Singer Sargent" made a valid point.

For Sargent and Hills, the significance of the critics' praise lies as much with portraiture as with watercolor, since each were both in a stylistically advancing manner, Sargent being as duly recognized as a painter of large society portraits as Hills was for her small, society portraits in miniature. And here we have a telling choice of iconography, for with it both artists have assumed analogous roles within their respective societies; both choosing to paint aristocratic portraits at a time when many other painters had turned toward more ordinary, even pedantic, subjects.

Still, beyond the similarity of theme, the qualities Hills' portraits share with Sargent's oil portraits, watercolors and pastels include a grandness of execution, occasionally attributed to the broad brushwork of the Dutch; overall, the refined ambiance associated with the sophisticate's world of finesse; revealing excursions into character; an enticingly sumptuous sense of design which leaves the viewer craving that second and third glance; a decorativeness associated with the graphic arts, and adaptations to French Impressionism.

Among the images of individuals, the broad based feeling in composition shares with the work of Sargent an ambiance rooted in the mutual admiration for the portrait style of a European painter of some import to Boston Impressionism, Carolus-Duran. While Sargent's exposure is directly traceable, having studied in France with Carolus-Duran, and Hills' is more indirect, possibly absorbing influences from Chase, Duveneck, Whistler or others associated with the Boston area milieu; the similarity is as perceivable as it is among the award winning portraits of other woman artists active amidst the environs of Boston. Boston seemed especially amenable to the aristocratic portrait tradition, and an underlying stylistic force originating with Carolus-Duran, characterized by the appearance of bravura brushstrokes, broadly "used to interpret both scintillating personalities and rich costumes of chic patrons of...society",[111] which has submerged within the boldly decisive feel of the Dutch, Fran Hals, combined with generous areas of bright, strong color contrasts, and innovations in angle, pose and background tending toward the informal carefully formalized, as if intended to reveal a casual depth of universal character nestled beneath aristocratic society's mandated silks. Hills does, though, refrain from indulging in compositions beholden to the Impressionist bird's-eye-view noted in works Sargent, doubtless due to such restraints of size as encumber the comparatively tiny ground of the miniature.

Both Sargent and Hills preferred painting slender ladies with delicate features and elongated bodies as presented a feminine image of grace inspired by the philosophy of Burke as has permeated pertinent segments of European and New England consciousness - witness the subtly endearing elegance of Hills' *"The Black Hat"*. Duran's French Impressionist mode of coloration mitigated through a subtle English consciousness favoring the restraint of local tones appropriately enlivened by glorious areas of scintillating accent colors common to Sargent, well reveals itself as a distinguishing characteristic of the miniatures of Hills, be it her *"Butterfly Girl"* or *"The Goldfish"*. Idiosyncratically, in her portraits of men, Hills is closer to Thomas Eakins' more darkly subtle renditions, as advance by comparison the emerging bright beacon of character as is reflected in the subject's visage.

Significantly, in their solitary sense of form, each artist reflects the influence of graphic media upon painting as innovations of Impressionism march forward toward Modernism through the increasing awareness and acceptance of areas of abstraction. For both Sargent and Hills, "sense" (empiricism), the verisimilitude of the natural world reigns supreme, and formal qualities of interpretation are subservient, though increasingly less so. It has been written that: "Emerging from important English precedent, the rise and increasing recognition of watercolor as an independent medium, accomplished through watercolor clubs, facilitated the acceptance of both watercolor and pastel as finished mediums."[112] Both watercolorists, Sargent's and Hills' sense of form partake of the end result of this acceptance, of empirical abstraction; Sargent predominantly in his watercolors on paper, Hills in her miniatures wherein at times her form exhibits the broad and bold decorativeness associated with the diffusive qualities of pigment immersed in water, the medium's transparent washes - and, of course, Hills' pastels.

The importance of watercolor to pastel's acceptance and character speaks to several of its mandates for Impressionist painters, since its opaque or dry washes and use of gouache share with the colored chalk as are pastels, the Impressionist dispersion of form, dissolution of color into broad areas of individually recognizable strokes, and the transposition of light into flat areas of abstract color whose transcriptions appear partially divorced from the volumetric rendering of realities of their underlying masses. These effects of flat color are heightened by the deliberate eschewal of half-tones in favor of shadows comprised of complementary hues, and, by the skirting of the edges of form with tints. Also present is the creation of reverse voids, a reverse space through which the underlying paper or ivory achieves the ascendancy of compositional form. For both artists, such techniques suggest hints of movement toward a love of Impressionism and beyond, a purist aesthetic of modern abstraction, as well as toward color harmonies emotively reflective of the interior thoughts of the private world of artists, as they shift toward the subjective or purely abstract art enticing painterly minds active at the turn of the twentieth century.

Hills' journey away from empiricism toward the flattening of form is characterized by a solitary linearity, absent in the work of Sargent. Hills' uncommon although not entirely unique, preferential use of linear outlining, rather than the conventional miniaturist's stippled contouring as circumscribes the broadly colored areas of her portrait miniatures, facilitates comparisons with Sargent's spatial breadth even as they remain idiosyncratically decorative after the manner of colored lithographs, which often appear as colored etchings with broadly outlined areas of bold, flat color.

Beyond Sargent's watercolors, the graphic arts may prove propitious partner to the art of pastels: for Hills worked as well as a book illustrator, designer of calendars and Valentine's Day cards, creator of embroidery designs and as a painter of decorative plate; all of which manner of creations stress the importance of line: independent, descriptive, and as a bounder of form. Hills' facility with contour linearity is not only historically unique among American miniatures, but significant since it aligns her work with American Impressionism, consequently distinguishing her work from the truly French Impressionist dissolution of form into abstract pieces with blurred contours, and as well, Barbizon and Tonalist works.

If Hills' interest in linearity occurs as the result of adherence to New England's tenets of truth to empirical naturalism as distinguish some segments of draftsmanly Boston Impressionism from its painterly French parent, such concerns conveniently coincide with Hills' co-exhibitor, the penultimate advocate of the workings of pure line, America's Linear Impressionist, Lilian Westcott Hale. While both these women artists share, as well, a love of nature and portraiture, in her miniatures and pastels Hills' sense of color remains perhaps more lyrical, partaking of the subtle sense of poetic rhythms.

Moreover, throughout the majority of her *oeuvre*, Hills is aligned with the conservative, tradition bound, Boston artists who enjoy Impressionism, but permit of no serious dalliances with either post-Impressionism or anything beyond it, including contemporaneous Modernist formulas. The reason for this may well be more political than aesthetic: Hills was, after all, essentially a New Englander, born and raised, and although clearly not Harvard University educated, certainly Brahmanized. By remaining true to the subculture of White, Anglo-Saxon, Protestant power brokers, and indeed her own background, Hills fit perfectly within the parameters of art which this source of clientele enjoyed and purchased. By so catering to her own subculture and its institutions, such as the National Academy of Design, the Guild of Boston Artists, the Copley Society, Hills enjoyed a well-planned and lucrative longevity. And, in these qualities, Hills is much like Hale and other Boston area women painters and miniaturists of this era with whom she exhibited; and therefore, most unlike New York artists or those working in various other regions of the country except possibly Philadelphia. The roots of this unifying affinity rests within the nineteenth rather than the twentieth century concept of the individual, and his place amidst other factors such as naturalism, lyricism, realism; and the fact that tradition-bound, conservative Boston Society preferred this nineteenth century, lyric individualism.

Hills' oeuvre *is* tradition bound - and very clearly so - if we think not in terms of one of the most telling, and obvious, of aesthetic variables - abstraction; but of an even more rudimentary, yet enlightening cultural variable, which is the changing concept and role of the individual. Not only is Hills' work concerned with conveying images of the singular, factual human being; but of all variables it is this preoccupation, this changing notion of individualism, which most concisely elucidates intra-century and inter-century underpinnings of change and differentiation. Further, the politics of individualism - the individualism of Whitman's nineteenth century - as coveted aesthetic ethos, politically *a propos* to Boston, helps explain Hills' immense popularity. The one portrait miniature exhibited nearby the next, as they all graced the exhibition halls of the Copley Society and the Guild of Boston Artists, doubtless, impressive portraits were they, the images created by Laura Coombs Hills.

HILLS AND THE PORTRAIT MINIATURE REVIVAL, 1890-1930:

"Having spearheaded the miniature revival
in the decades preceding and following 1900..."

Sandra B. Lepore

So begins the second line of Lepore's article "Breaking the Accepted Rules of Color"[113] in which she pinpoints Laura Coombs Hills' role as a dominant one in the miniature revival occurring in America at the turn of the twentieth century.

Further, author and art historian Maryanne Sudnick Gunderson, looking through the lens of the twenty-first century, in her thesis of 2003 entitled *"Diminished yet Disarming: The Portrait Miniature Revival, 1890-1930"*, adds numerous insights into the changes occurring during the era in which Hills created her miniatures. Yet first she notes that the traditional miniature was "a fresh but simple image translated through a medium to light color scheme and subtle background...Brushwork was unique to this traditional miniature; both stippling and cross-hatching were best for applying watercolor pigment to the slightly matte, ivory surface."[114]

Yet, as we contemplate Hills' miniatures we note that, uniquely, she utilized not stippling as recommended as early as T. S. Cummings' article, but line more similar to that found in the graphic arts. Hills' is a type of line drawn with linear contours bordering broad areas of much stronger and bolder color - much like chromolithography - with which Hills would have been very familiar as an employee of Louis Prang Chromolithographers. In addition Hills' color scheme possesses the vibrancy and drama of the theatre.

As Gunderson informs us: "Women artists were, in fact, involved in key historic advancements of the art form."[115] And she states: "By the early 1800s, the miniature profession thrived throughout the United States."[116]

Gunderson then explains that: "A major shift in its [the miniature's] artistry, however, occurred about 1890. The expressed shift included changes in color, size, shape, patronage, and even the type of artist involved..."[117] Further, she elucidates her assessment of the potential reasons for these changes, some of which include: 1) the Arts and Crafts and Art Nouveau philosophies which advocated the "hand-crafted object of abstracted forms and colors" and led to miniatures being utilized as table portraits; 2) "the American portraiture of John Singer Sargent and Mary Cassatt and the French artist Edgar Degas...in the area of brushwork, new compositional devices..." which led to the influence of pastels on miniatures; 3) the emergence of photography...

which appears to have actually contributed to the miniature revival..." "...since patrons preferred the more idealized version of themselves presented in [the more expensive] miniatures"; 4) the emergence of the revivalist miniaturist such as Eulabee Dix, who working c. 1895, avoided the traditional use of weak colors and harsh stippling - which led to "new interests" now being referred to as the Miniature Revival, dating c. 1890-1930; and 5) the increasing role of New York's Greenwich Village as an artistic center, as Gunderman observes that Boston changes to a literary location.[118]

Interestingly, she informs us that: "Laura Coombs Hills' colorful, pictorial style represented perhaps the obvious link between Tiffany, Art Nouveau, and the Miniature Revival"[119] doubtless in the abstracted forms from Nature adapted from the jewelry and furniture screen designs of the time and the vibrant color scheme, which yielded an effect that was comparatively modern. As Gunderson explains: "The Black Mantle...[reveals] the loose, painterly brushwork is confined largely to the abstract background."[120]

Further, the author observes that American Impressionists and contemporary miniaturists had much in common: "...Appropriately, Laura Coombs Hills exhibited with Frank Weston Benson, William Merritt Chase, Childe Hassam, and Joseph Decamp in Maine where Hills' work showed the influence of "Weston [Benson], Chase, and Hassam, with the blurring of backgrounds, brighter colors, Japanese prints and peculiar shadowing of the face which Hills incorporated for years to come."[121]

Moreover, assimilating the celebratory spirit of early American precedents in portraiture, and the creative palette of twentieth century color employed to reflect personality, Hills miniatures appear both traditional and innovative. As icons of American Lyricism, they conspire to advance themes associated with Sense and Sensibility, by which is meant in the case of the former: reason, empiricism, civil law society, and natural verisimilitude; and by the latter: sentiment, romance, poetics, beauty, and the triggering of an aesthetic response.

Generally, Hills' miniatures remain endearingly daring in pose, background and color, while maintaining a characteristic New England reserve and standard of taste wherein, as the critics confirm for us, resides much of their appeal.

By reviving miniatures, Hills brought to the fore the underlying sentiments surrounding their original usage and initial associations common around the time of the American Civil War, when these artistic and psychological gemstones existed as icons, not only of men's romantic love for and appreciation of women, but equally important, of all other associated values of American brotherhood: family, country, love, honor, romance. With her art, Hills, the twentieth century artist, revived not only the dying seeds of conservative values of an earlier century; not only an ancestral art form; and hence, an American pictorialization of both indigenous American and inherited English poetics; but through nurture and encouragement, brought to fruition a particular ethos of sentiment and individualism inherent in American culture, for perhaps its last resurgence before its retreat into obscurity in the face of Modernism's ever more powerful technological, abstract, secular presence. And, the critics, as we will see, loved her work.

The Critics

Laura Coombs Hills

THE old saying that artists, like poets, are born, not made, is verified in the career of Laura Coombs Hills, who without question ranks among the leading miniature painters of today.

It was just twenty-two years ago that Miss Hills painted her first miniature. She had been in England on a visit and a young English girl, seeing some of her work, had asked her why she did not like to paint miniatures. Her reply was that she did not think she would like to. But under persuasion she had purchased some little pieces of ivory and brought them home with her intending to make some experiments. Up to that time she had done some illustrating and decorative painting, work on china and in commercial design, good work, but not of a kind supposedly advancing. Back in Newburyport, her home, Miss Hills set to work, secured some young girls to sit for her and employed her medium as best she could. The result was amazing. In a very short time seven miniatures were completed and a new vital personality in the world of art discovered. For from the moment Miss Hills took up miniature painting, she stood, not only alone, but in the forefront of those in this field of endeavor, coming as it were, full-fledged into her own.

She had no traditions, she had not studied the miniatures of earlier masters. She selected her own road and followed it fearlessly. Her expression was perfectly natural and at the same time simple, and although it has since been improved and refined, it is today much as it was then, broad, frank, and very individual. Obviously, Miss Hills had genius, that inborn gift without which no amount of training can really avail. She had, furthermore, industry and a keen sense of values. She saw clearly and was not afraid. Competition naturally stimulates effort, but it sometimes leads to confusion. Miss Hills was mercifully saved from the self-consciousness so often, unluckily, bred by art school life. Her outlook was impersonal, unhampered, genuine. She had something to do and she did it as well as she could, the way it seemed to her it should be done. That this way coincided fundamentally with that followed by those in the past who had achieved success was not mere accident, but rather proof of the universality of art, the common basis upon which art at its best is built.

Miss Hills not only sees clearly and accurately, but has what is essential to portrait painting, real insight into character, and she is heartily in sympathy with her fellows. People interest her and she is quick in discerning their real individuality. To this trait of character some of her success as a portrait painter may well be attributed.

She also has a fine sense of color and her miniatures are not infrequently primarily color schemes, painted with the purpose of setting forth lovely harmonies and contrasts. She paints broadly, less so than at first but still more broadly than the majority, yet her miniatures never have the appearance of haste, nor do they lack finish. The color is as a rule applied in broad washes and is clear and vital. Sometimes it is rich and dark, at other times sparkling and delicate, but it is always in effect transparent and the lovely tone of the ivory beneath is invariably preserved.

There is nothing photographic about Miss Hills' miniatures. Though they are small in dimensions (about the size of the reproductions given herewith) they are large in effect, and the mere matter of size is forgotten - the work in itself is big and strong, and it is that which signifies.

The people she paints, moreover, are real people, individual, vivid, not mere puppets posing, nor fashion plates. She has exceptional success in securing satisfactory likenesses without in even the smallest degree sacrificing the demands of art. Her portraits are intimate and yet at the same time dignified. They have that quality which may be designated as style, but they are subtle and reticent. In other words, they are essentially human, many-sided, real interpretations of character and personality seen and interpreted by one possessing both sympathy and individuality. For distinction in portraiture is derived not alone most often from the sitter, but from the painter, the recorder, who is of course all this and much more.

Miss Hills' miniatures (and she painted over 200), have pictorial quality which is a little unusual and very charming. As large canvases rendered in oils, they would be found decorative and impressive. Not a few suggest action, as for example, *"Daffodils"*, but they are never restless. In the painting of children Miss Hills has been especially successful, but her miniatures of men and women (children of fuller years) are no less satisfying nor sympathetic. The reproductions given herewith go to show the wide range of her achievement.

Miss Hills as a rule spends her summers in Newburyport and her winters in Boston. She is a tireless worker, painting every forenoon whether she has orders or not, loving her work and going to it invariably with enthusiasm, that she brings to her play. She is a boon companion and valued friend, one who will always retain the joyousness of youth, looking upon life itself as a great adventure, and going out to meet it with courage and expectation, that expectation which would and usually does discover something delightful at each new turning of the road.

She has exhibited in London and frequently in this country, and has received not only the highest commendation for her work but numerous much coveted awards.

Miss Hills became a member of the Society of American Artists in 1897, and an associate member of the National Academy of Design in 1906. She is also a member of the American Society of Miniature Painters, of the Copley Society and the Guild of Boston Artists.[122]

L.M. (Leila Mechlin)
American Magazine of Art

Her studio on Boylston Street, Boston, is a very attractive place, for she shows here that decorative talent that is so prominent in all her work. The interior is finished in dark green and gold, the artist's favorite combination, and is filled with deliciously quaint furniture and rare bric-a-brac. On the walls are the originals of the numerous friends in the profession, Mildred Howells, Oliver Herford, Ethel Reed, and many others.

Personally, Miss Hills is delightful to meet; an interesting brunette of medium height, with a decided faculty for making one feel most welcome in her presence, and an inexhaustible sense of fun. A strong spirit of enterprise shows in everything she does. No trouble is too great if there is an effect to produce and her hands can produce it. The accompanying illustrations show some of her most characteristic work in the field where she has made her greatest success. It is to be regretted that the exquisite color cannot be reproduced.[123]

(April, 1899; Vol. V; No. 3)

"...the first miniature painter to be elected to the Society of American Artists. Although never taught miniature painting, Miss Hills is recognized as a most skillful painter and has gained honors both at home and abroad in this particular form of art.

Her first exhibit was "Seven Pretty Girls at Newburyport." *"The Bride"*, a harmony in gray, gold and blue, was one of the most evanescently delicate pieces at a recent exhibition. *"The Black Mantle"*, *"Fire Opal"*, *"Butterfly"*, and *"Goldfish"* represent the most modern development of all, the essentially pictorial miniature. In these fanciful subjects she takes a place among colorists of the first rank. Her miniature of Alice Brown is full of insight and penetration; the portrait of Mr. Arthur Harlow has all the breadth and dignity of a large portrait with the charm peculiar to the miniature; the charming little head of Dorothy S. is frank and altogether lovely; the portrait of little Miss Hale is as wholly delightful a child portrait as one could ask.

Frances Duncan in writing of Miss Hills' work said: "Her portraits are not large portraits done small, but essentially miniature; they have an exquisite jewel-like quality peculiar to the miniature in the hands of the few masters of this exquisite and lovely art, the quality which will make miniature painting a thing apart."

"She understands the emotion of color and by a graceful dexterity masters its adaptation to its subject."

Her portraits are always big in conception and she appears to be little hampered by the tiny brushes and the elusive quality of the ivory."

The portrait of Master Donald Moffat was the *chef d'oeuvre* at a recent exhibition of the Miniature Society.

Her masterpiece, *"The Black Hat"*, is owned by the Metropolitan Museum, New York.

Alice T. Searle says: "Miss Hills is never dull but in the center one of her group of three large ovals (at a recent exhibition), the *Portrait of Miss Isabel da Costa Green*, she outshone her own brilliant past."

In referring to an exhibition of miniature work by American painters held in Boston last year, the Boston Transcript says of Miss Hills' contributions: "A truly remarkable group. In it are outstanding examples of the personal style which is this artist's unique contribution to contemporary practice in miniature painting - the personal style that is so full of elegance and distinction, of such charm and fine taste, and allowing for the diminutive scale, of such astonishing breadth and decorative character."

Her painting has some of Sargent's own qualities of dexterous swiftness, her likenesses an assurance and an apparent ease which are his, too. Her mastery of her medium indeed is beyond comparison with any other living painter except with Sargent himself. As John Alexander once said on looking at a miniature of hers, "Never since Holbein-" and a silence more eloquent than words finished his sentence."

Miss Hills is placed in the highest rank among artists who have distinguished themselves in miniature work in the United States."[124]

Newspaper excerpts reproduced in
American Artists, Biographical Sketches

...Miss Hills is a prominent and successful miniaturist, and her numerous pictures are in the possession of her subjects...decidedly individual in character, no matter how simple her arrangements, she gives her pictures a cachet of distinction...whether a lady in a black gown with a black aigrette in her hair and a background of delicate turquoise blue, or the delicate profile of a red-haired beauty, outlined against tapestry, or the snowy head and shoulders rising out of dusty brown velvet; the effect is gem-like, a revelation of exquisite coloring that is entirely artistic...portrait of a little lady apparently six or seven years old, in an artistic old fashioned gown, the bodice low in neck and out in sharp point at the waistline in front, elbow sleeves, slippers with large rosettes, just peeping out from her dress, her feet not touching the floor, so high is she seated. Her hair curling about her face, is held back by a ribbon bandeau in front; one long, heavy curl rests on the left side of her neck, and is surmounted by a big butterfly bow. The costume and pose are delightful and striking at first, but the more the picture is studied the more the face attracts the attention it merits. It is a sweet little girl's face, modest and sensible. She is holding the arm of her seat with determination but her expression shows that she is thinking of other things that she intends to do as soon as she can.[125]

Unknown source

...Laura Coombs Hills, one of the best miniature painters in the country, is represented by a group of veritable masterpieces...In each the color scheme is a joy, and the group upon the walls of the Guild (of Boston Artists} gallery glow like jewels. Her *"Daffodils"* is all in the basket of flowers carried by the young woman, all being in yellow. It is full of action.

Beautiful pieces of color and painting also are her *"Miss Belle Da Costa Green"* and *"Portrait of Miss Maude Appleton."*[126]

Journal, May 4, 1915.

"...By far the most interesting exhibit of miniatures that have been shown in Boston for some time is to be seen this week at the Artist's Guild. There are in all some 125 miniatures displayed comprising six separate groups by as many artists, each of which would make a show well worth visiting.

Without doubt the finest little paintings are those by Laura Coombs Hills, who is today one of the most able miniature painters in the country. To those who little realize the possibilities of miniature painting her work must ever prove a revelation, for it shows all the "big" qualities of portrait painting on large canvases and yet retains all its proper delicacy and charm...Miss Hills is fond of using a dominant color note in each portrait that lends it a distinct decorative value. One of the best is of *Mrs. G.W. Chadwick*, a composition of violet reds in various combinations harmoniously enframing an excellent bit of portraiture. Equally characterized by its color scheme of blue and blacks is the painting of *Edith Harlow* with its graceful and natural figure pose. Most striking in coloring is the portrait of *Miss Ruth Graves*, a young girl, in black in a chair of bright yellow against a background of even brighter yellow. An effective Oriental composition is the portrait of *Miss Belle Da Costa Greene*, showing a decided brunette wrapped in a vivid orange-red veil. Two other delightful color harmonies are the portrait of *Barbara Bartlett* in golds and pinks and *"Daffodils"*, a decorative figure in yellows."[127]

Providence Journal, May 16, 1916

"...The art event of the week is the opening of the miniature exhibition in the Guild of Boston Artists with examples - one hundred or more - by six well-known Boston painters - the Misses Hills, Cross, Purdie, Hawley, Coolidge, and Oliver.

The small portraits have been hung in groups, each united rather than separated, by a series of Japanese decorations of old and gentle tones.

If true, as has been said, that "Genius is the capacity for taking intimate pains" the painting of rare miniatures might well be regarded as a manifestation of something like genius, since for no worker in the fine arts is it more necessary to develop this capacity than for the miniatures. The skill of the modern miniaturist, as well as the present day point of view, is well-proven by this exhibition. Miss Laura Hills' group on the East wall is very handsome, with its 20 examples of rich and beautiful color combinations, graceful and decisive line, and sympathetic interpretation of character.

One notes (with gratitude of a new color scheme) the portrait of Miss Harlow, a distinguished presentation of the New England type. The head is wonderfully well-painted, and dominates the white arrangement, which is in subtly contrasted tones of rich black and a queer, remote, gray-green. Another remarkable work by this painter is called *"Daffodils"*, a figure of buoyant grace of action and delectable colors."[128]

Advertiser, May 6, 1915

"...The miniature exhibition, tastefully arranged with Japanese accessories, gives a favorable impression of the status of this branch of art of painting. Bar Malbone, hardly any of the American portraitists who flourished before Daguerre spoiled their trade, could make so thoroughly artistic a likeness as can our Miss Hills. The blight of Academicism that sticks out over many contemporary English miniatures, is apparent in none of the Guild's group.

Laura Coombs Hills is a veritable John Sargent of miniature painting, and one instinctively turns to her display knowing it will be marked by original gesture and posture, brilliant color, precise and intense characterization. Miss Hills' work is always definitive and distinguished; sometimes one feels in it the formula by which it is made, though that is not necessarily to the detriment of a work of art. There is something cheerfully stimulating in the rich red garments and red violet backgrounds that are strikingly alike in the likeness of Mrs. George W. Chadwick and Miss Maude E. Appleton. Among the other successful ones is that of Miss Louis Graves."[129]

Herald, May 9, 1915

"...The success of the Guild of Boston Artists has become an accepted fact. It has a handsome and well-arranged clubhouse on Newbury Street, near the Boston Art Club...its forty active members include many of the most prominent artists in the community, while its associate membership of 350 is drawn from the best known local art connoisseurs. Two galleries occupy the lower floor of the building, one to be used as a general exhibition place for the series of "one-man" shows, to be given fort-nightly during the year. A private gallery on the second floor will contain miscellaneous works, sketches, studies, etc. by the artist members.

An exhibition of works by the active members of the Guild has been in progress for two weeks, each member showing one or more examples, the four miniaturists contributing a group each. As an exhibition of modern work and of the so-called various artists, the work throughout is marked by unusual technical excellence, and although a general show can hardly be expected to be of uniform merit, "the talent of the amateur" is nowhere in evidence.

(The article goes on to describe the works of other contributing artists.)...The miniaturists make an interesting corner and prove that "portraits in little" can be pictures as well, even within the limitations of a few inches. Miss Hills' *"Portrait of Mrs. Chadwick"*, Miss Margaret Hawleys' study of a youth, Miss Sally Cross', *"Portrait of Mrs. G."* and Miss Jean Oliver's *"Good Morning"*, a study of a little child, are all excellent examples of this fascinating art."[130]

Boston Herald, March 7, 1915

"It is doubtful if there is another city in the country that could produce a group of miniature painters equal to the six Boston women who are exhibiting their work... Ever since women have taken up seriously the profession of painting they have been steadily superseding men in this field.

One distinguishing characteristic of this latter-day miniature painting is in the way of color contrasts for these artists, but somehow it nearly always results in a beautiful harmony.

Take for instance the portrait of *Mrs. G.W. Chadwick* by Laura Coombs Hills. It required the nerve of a major painter to introduce that red shawl over shoulders and body and hope to paint the head in such a way that it would not be subordinated. There is character and expression in every outline. It is a masterpiece.

The portrait of *Miss Barbara Bartlett* by the same artist is another triumph. The blonde hair, blue eyes, and the whole refined personal charm of the young woman are blended and glorified. *"The Blue Bandeau"* is a beautiful miniature of a young woman by Miss Hills, a profile exquisite in every detail and texture.

....Of making many miniatures there is no end. The vogue of these little portraits on ivory appears to be going on stronger than ever...In a general way the quality of this collection is much above the average, and it is apparent that the contributors have chosen only their best productions to represent them. This, in fact, has been a notable feature of all the Guild exhibitions up to date, and it accounts for the gratifying artistic success of the first season of the new organization.

Miss Hills' group of works will naturally engage the attention of the visitor first of all, because of her great reputation, which has been won by intrinsic merit. The scale on which she elects to paint nowadays is rather larger than the traditional miniatures; and for this she doubtless has good reason; she makes many figures nearly full length, for one thing, and does not confine herself to head alone. Miss Hills has not precisely revolutionized the genre, but her example has been on the whole influential in the direction of modifying the practice of the American miniaturists, so that the somewhat anemic color scheme formerly regarded with favor has given place to a richer and more resourceful palette. She has the "decorative sense" so much talked about and likes to deal with brilliant stuffs and colorful backgrounds as accessories to her likenesses.

Indeed, many of her miniatures are frankly decorative and more or less ideal figures rather than portraits; such works are her *"Daffodils"* and *"The Blue Bandeau"* in the present exhibition, which are very effective and delightful compositions. On the whole she has achieved an enlargement of the scope of the miniatures by her inventiveness and audacious employment of color. But if one would judge her qualities as a portraitist, the likeness of *Miss Edith Harlow*, one of her recent works, testifies eloquently to her power of rendering personal character and giving to her sister the stamp of individuality. In character reading, this is one of her masterpieces. The head is wonderfully painted. Was it not a mistake, however, to hide the right hand in the muff, giving the disagreeable, if monetary impression of an amputation?"[131]

Transcript, May 1915

"...Preliminary inspection of a few photographs of the miniatures to be shown indicate that the showing will be of high quality as well as ample quantity. A notable contribution is Miss Hills' portrait of *Miss Ruth Graves*, seated in a chintz chair, with straw hat held loosely in the left hand, and the right hand thrown over the side of the chair."[132]

Boston Herald, May 2, 1915

"Another daring portrait in its color contrasts by Miss Hills is that of *Miss Belle Da Costa Greene*, famous as the youthful, vivacious and competent librarian of the late J. Pierpont Morgan."[133]

Boston Globe, May 1915

"...It is evident that the Boston group of miniatures have, one and all, put their best feet foremost in this brilliant show.

(The exhibition) is furthermore an interesting sort of social register which a gathering of miniatures of this character assembles. Here are representative men, women, and children, who will, no doubt treasure the little pictures made on ivory in 1921 even as people of this generation give a place of honor in the home to the likeness of grandfather and grandmother who at the time of their marriage in the 1920s came up to Boston and had their miniatures painted.

Here, in Miss Hills' very artistic and beautiful group are the portraits of Mrs. Samuel Cabot and daughter, Nancy, Miss Concuelo Bates, Mrs. Vincent Goldthwaite, Mrs. Albert Titcomb, Henry Robbins, Chadwick Wiggins, Miss Jane Everett, Mrs. Matthew J. Whittall, Cola Rossai, Miss Marian Nutter, Miss Katherine Everett, Viola Wilson, Miss Ruth Graves, Mrs. Lewis Parkhurst, Philip Morgan, Mr. and Mrs. Louis Drake, Miss Prudence Drake, Miss Laura Drake, Marion Wood, Miss Grace Smith, Miss Helen Smith."[134]

Unknown newspaper

"MODERN AMERICAN MINIATURE PAINTERS
by Lucia Fairchild Fuller

...American painters began to experiment with water color on ivory. Laura Coombs Hills was first of these new painters publicly to appear when, early in the winter of 1894, at a gallery in Boston, she held an exhibition of some few miniatures which she painted the preceding months. So immediate was her success that before the exhibition closed she had received no less than twenty-seven commissions for portrait miniatures.

...in New York: William J. Baer showed his group of miniatures...in Paris, Alice Beckington painted miniatures...in Cambridge, Massachusetts, Theodora W. Thayer displayed miniatures...the demand for miniatures became so great and as must always happen, inferior painters crowded so rapidly into the field, that in 1898 William Baer felt himself actually obliged to found the American Society of Miniature Painters in order to protect the ideals of the newly revived old art. Every year since, this society has held exhibitions: first at Knoedler's Galleries; then with the National Academy of Design, recently at Arden Studios...These painters believed in painting from life (no photographs) ...shows reverence for nature and of belief in guidance by the trained and seeing eye...The new quality which these two painters (Hills and Alice Beckington) along with their friends, have added to the old art is the naturalistic approach, after all...the hallmark of their time. While they kept the delicacy and finesse of treatment of far earlier days, they painted their sitters in modern dress and in their own surroundings. They broke away from the "sky background" and the floating scarf which had been imposed by Cosway...Bright radiant color of Miss Hills is far more easily understood (than the color of Alice Beckington). Her painting has some of Sargent's own qualities of dexterous swiftness, her likenesses an assurance and an apparent ease which are his too. Her mastery of her medium indeed, is beyond comparison with any other living painter except with Sargent himself.[135]

Scribner's Magazine, 1920.

ARTS AND ARTISTS, Dorothea Lawrence Mann, Editor,
Published by a group of members of the Boston Art Club.

LAURA COOMBS HILLS

"PERHAPS the most eagerly awaited exhibition each year is that of Laura Coombs Hills, and incidentally, the one bringing the most sales, for, in the leanest years of depression, at least three-fourths of her pictures always sold. Previous to this an eager public would gather before the gallery and when the doors opened would dash in and toward a picture - any picture - place their hand upon it and feel fortunate to have reached it first. Within a few minutes all would be sold.

Miss Hills' proficiency has come through concentrated work rather than formal instruction, having had but a few months of the latter.

Inspired to try miniatures, when told in London that it was simply "watercolors on ivory", she secured some pieces and returning to Newburyport painted seven miniatures with which she held her first exhibition, vibrant with life and color. Twenty-two orders resulted and from this beginning she rose to become our foremost miniature painter.

A lover of flowers, she has always drawn or painted them. Her first flower pastel was purchased by Sarah Orne Jewett who wrote enthusiastically that Miss Hills had captured the soul of the flower in her painting.

Miss Hills stresses order and neatness, "no place in art for slipshod, careless work," she says. Her thousands of crayons in orderly rows; a shallow box receives those being used until the picture is finished when they are dusted and returned to their original boxes. With her composition planned and picture visualized she "plunges in" and for two hours works with a concentration that blots out all else - and - she never has a failure. For strong contrast powerful electric lights are used; pink and green make her vibrant grays; one color is sometimes brushed lightly over another for veiling, and her little finger is her most valued tool. Backgrounds are modeled as carefully as the subject. Such brilliancy of color as she achieves is almost unique with Miss Hills. Her gorgeous backgrounds never detract from her subject, such a master of relative color balance is she. French pastel board or pastel canvas, with crayons from Paris or New York are used, and never any fixatif. Instinctive with her are the mechanics of painting, thus her work is always spontaneous.

Meeting Miss Hills, one is impressed with her eager aliveness. This quality transmitted to her paintings makes them pulsate with life.

Miss Hills credits her sister with the magic beauty. She also solves domestic problems, giving Miss Hills the freedom so necessary to the accomplishment of artistic ideals. "God bless a single sister."[136]

Florence Spaulding, December 1936

THE MINIATURES OF MISS LAURA HILLS
By Frances Duncan

FROM her first exhibition of miniatures, the work of Laura Coombs Hills has always been peculiarly interesting and refreshingly individual.

Miss Hills was born in the old seaport town of Newburyport; her academic training was exceedingly slight - some work during three winters in the studio of Miss Helen M. Knowlton, in Boston, three months in New York at the Art Students' League, where she was in the portrait class of William Merritt Chase, and two months at the Cowles Art School. She was never taught miniature painting - it is interesting, almost amusing, to note that of our miniaturists those whose work is of the most enduring worth were never "taught" that particular form of art.

Some fourteen years ago miniature painting occupied a small and not very brilliantly lighted corner in the field of American art. The only miniaturists of note were Mr. Baer, now President of the American Society of Miniature Painters, and Mr. Josephi. The miniature was still the miniature of tradition, a detailed, polished little painting; in fact, so carefully polished as almost to shine. For with the miniature, as happens with other forms of art when in need of a revival, the form of the earlier masters was followed without their vitality, the mold without their breath of life. Instead, of using their footprints on the sands of time simply to indicate the direction, artists were still carefully and laboriously stepping.

It was at this time, at a slender exhibition of miniatures, that Laura Hills made her first appearance, exhibiting a little group, the portraits of Seven Pretty Girls of Newburyport. Into the heavy atmosphere of correct, conventional miniature painting the entrance of these little ivories, warm and aglow with life and color, fresh and new in their viewpoint, sincere with an almost naive sincerity, was like a breath of fresh air in an overheated drawing room or the wind on the dry bones of Ezekiel's vision.

Since then miniature painting has won for itself a fiery definite place in American art. There are the few who are doing beautiful and enduring work - for the past dozen years have brought to the front such artists as Mrs. Fuller, Miss Alice Beckington, the late Theodora Thayer, whose work was marvelously full of character and charm; there are also the many who follow in their train at a greater or lesser distance, for the wide-flung doors of the miniature exhibitions seem almost as Catholic in their welcome to newcomers as those of Ellis Island. But one can always turn to Miss Hills' work with a sense of positive refreshment. Her painting has, of course, become more varied, more subtle, wider in its scope, but, although having gained in depth and vigor, her work has never lost its unhesitating directness, its delightful spontaneity.

Miss Hills is a born miniaturist. Her portraits are not large portraits done small, but essentially miniatures; they have that exquisite jewel-like quality peculiar to the miniature in the hands of the few masters of this exquisite and lovely art, the quality which will always make miniature painting a thing apart. Also, she has a wonderful sense of scale; her miniatures could neither be smaller nor larger without missing some of their point, losing something of their perfectness.

In her painting she always gives one the impression of knowing precisely what she wants to do and doing it with ease and sureness; of having something to say in art and saying it with force and certainty.

There is nothing of feminine timidity, never any mere prettiness; her work is strong, vital, large (except in actual inches) and never monotonous; in fact, in Miss Hills one expects the unexpected. Her color is peculiarly fresh and clear, and pure in tone; never does it look worried out of its integrity by a changing purpose in the artist. It is probable that the rapidity with which she works, the comfortable faculty of knowing exactly what she wishes to do, has something to do with this delightful quality in her color.

Her backgrounds show astonishing inventiveness and resourcefulness, and the relation of the sitter to the background is a thing which from her receives evidently very careful study; and yet, original and daring as she often is here, she never gives one the impression of being intentionally unusual; daring; daring effects in color are never used for the sake of astonishing folk, but to accomplish a definite artistic purpose. Take, for instance, her well-known *Flame Girl* - the intense background brings out the cool, pure color of the face with an almost dramatic value, very effective, but few artists would have thought of it, which is one reason why this miniature attracted so much attention, though I doubt if Miss Hills herself considered it very unusual; to her it was a most natural thing to do. There is always a refreshing variety in her composition. It is a far cry from the *Butterfly Girl*, a thing of exquisite, light and filmy delicacy - of "wingy mysteries", Sir Thomas Browne would say - to the portrait of *Persis Blair*, in which even the background echoes the quaint seriousness of the wholly delightful child figure.

It is this originality in scheme and composition, this almost dramatic instinct, which has made her work as a painter of portraits less noticed, perhaps than for its decorative beauty. That is, the expression of her own personality has interested folk more than her ability to express the personality of another, which is a different thing.

In fact, this imaginative quality frequently gets the upper hand in her painting and her intention seems to find what decorative thing she can make out of her sitter, rather than to discover what manner of person he is and bring this forth on the ivory; to fit him, or more likely her, into a preconceived color scheme rather than to fit her scheme to the personality of her sitter. This is more noticeable in the later work than in the earlier; at all events, one sometimes wishes she would take out the artist's license and paint a purely imaginative thing - Lamia, or Isabella with her pot of basil, or Puck on a dragon fly, and then, having satisfied her decorative instinct, paint a portrait pure and simple. For Miss Hills can paint portraits. Her miniature of *Alice Brown* is full of insight and penetration. The portrait of *Mr. Arthur Harlow* has all the breadth and dignity of a large portrait with the charm peculiar to the miniature. There is the charming little head of *Dorothy S.*, frank and altogether lovely; the miniature of Miss S., and the portrait of little *Miss Hale* of the last exhibition is as wholly delightful a child portrait as one could ask.[137]

For in Miss Hills there is that uncompromising truthfulness of the New Englander, although her interest in texture, in color and in composition makes this not always prominent; nonetheless, it is an underlying quality and again and again comes out strongly in her portraits.

Miss Hills was the first miniature painter elected to the Society of American Artists.[138]

International Studio, 1910

She treats them (her miniatures) much as a Lilliputian might a life-sized portrait with free handling on a tiny scale, using fine lines in her background where others stipple - a departure from custom that has stamped her work as belonging to a new school.[139]

(She is) comparatively self-taught - her method has been of her own development.[140]

She has a wonderful sense of scale, her miniatures could neither be smaller nor larger without missing some of their point, losing something of their perfection.[141]

(Her work has) the breadth and dignity of a large portrait with the charm peculiar to the miniature.[142]

These...(are) secretly, cheerfully stimulating alike in the rich red garments and red violet backgrounds that (are) as strikingly alike in the likeness of *Mrs. George*

*Witherdernick, of Miss Maude E. Appleton...*Among the other successful ones is Miss Louis Graves.[143]

(Her) portraits are big in conception.[144]

...elegance, distinction, charm, fine taste...[145]

...astonishing breadth and decorative character...[146]

...revelation of exquisite coloring...[147]

...owes her pre-eminence to an especial line...[148]

...A veritable John Singer Sargent of miniature painting and one instinctively turns to her display knowing that it will be marked by original gesture and posture, brilliant color, precise and intense characterization...[149]

Section Three:

Perfect Pastels and The Critics

Perfect Pastels

PERFECT PASTELS: THE CULTURAL MILIEU:

As a pastelist, Laura Coombs Hills inspires us for a variety of reasons. Through her portrayal of portraits of flowers, Hills' oeuvre offers us a solitary opportunity to glimpse insights reflective of the history of America's cultural values and changing artistic milieu, as snippets of its ideational evolution are transformed into splendid visual images.

The study of Hills' art is not merely the study of a dually talented miniaturist and pastelist; but an interesting tale of personal artistic growth and tenacity, glittering like a diamond as it unfolds against a multifaceted backdrop of contemporaneous art historical developments and a preceding century's cultural trends; whose underlying concepts, in their uncanny ability to persevere, present us with an elegant elocution of the most stalwart of American values. Like the writer, Whitman, Hills' remarkable work reflects an ethos garnered from the merger of ideas gleaned from literary, artistic, and political worlds peculiar to the late nineteenth and early decades of the twentieth century in America, and transformed into a uniquely expressed aesthetic, a type of "Democratic Aesthetic Naturalism" married to a regional Lyrical Impressionism, clearly audible to all Americans.

Further, her work represents a significant step in the evolution of America's national pastel tradition: a lively and exemplary terminus to aesthetic discussions concerning the innate worthiness of the medium, its significance, and the impact of the intermingling of watercolors and pastels. Hills' pastels played a part in the decorative arts impact upon the vital sister of the fine arts - oil painting - begun in the nineteenth century, and culminating in a final transition toward unwavering, categorical acceptance of the pastel medium as a finished rather than merely preliminary art form. If Hills' pastels fail to represent the earliest moment during which pastels were crowned full-fledged members in the exclusive and coveted circle of the fine arts of architecture, painting and sculpture; then ever cognizant of the solitary influences in Hills' background as facilitated the espousal of their primary decorative tendencies, her pastels stand ready, proudly representing some of their common crown's finest, most vibrant jewels.

Since, as a rule, American pastelists chose to represent a subject matter identical to the country's American miniaturists: portraiture, similar to Hills' own small, ivory treasures; Hills' pastels blossom uniquely in their floral iconography. Her flower pastels are equally individual yet derivative, representational yet representative, empirical and naturalistic yet iconic. The underlying structure of Hills' pastels bear multiple faces and as such singly within the broader scope of world culture, Hills' *oeuvre* combines the tripartite influences of French, English and American origins; manipulating thematic facets plucked from all in a quest to develop her own distinctive style intended to transform tidbits into timeless symbols.

And in their appeal to patrons and collectors, Hills' flower pastels were and are timeless. Beginning with her serious devotion to pastel production during the 1920s, continuing during the Depression of the 1930s, and the ensuing decades until the current moment, Hills' flower pastels were always in demand by galleries such as Boston's Doll and Richards, and The Copley Society; and by individual patrons as well. Indeed, during the Depression years, her pastels typically sold for $100.00 to $500.00 dollars each[150]. Today, 100 years after the roaring twenties, her pastels sell predominantly according to three respective tiers: those images costing $3,000.00 to $5,000.00 such as *Night Blooming Cereus*; those selling for $8,000.00 to $20,000.00 such as *Zinnias in a Green Bowl*, and *Tulips on Chintz*; and finally, those which can be purchased for from $20,000.00 to $50,000.00 such as *Still-life with White Gladiolas and Blue Delphinium, Still-life with Larkspur and Glass Orb, Jonquils and Narcissus*, and *Heavenly Blues - A Still-life with Morning Glories*. (Meanwhile, her miniatures generally cost between $3,000.00 and $6,000.00; and sold for $1,000.00 during the Depression.)[151]

Moreover, the continued longevity of the popularity of Hills' flower pastels is truly remarkable considering the number of decades during which she produced these beautiful bouquets, and the variety of new aesthetic developments and trends occurring (and competing for sales dollars) during Hills' lifetime. Indeed, her first works were sold during the very prosperous "roaring twenties" in America, a decade which was replete with themes of sexuality, technology, and social progress and *avant-garde* developments in the arts. It was the era of flappers, the Harlem Renaissance and F. Scott Fitzgerald's "Jazz Age", writers such as Ernest Hemingway, William Faulkner and Andre Breton; psychoanalysis and Salvador Dali; the subjective perspective of Expressionism and Wassily Kandinsky; and American painters such as Realist George Luks and abstract nature artist, Georgia O'Keefe.[152]

Then, during the ensuing great Depression of the 1930s, America searched for a new identity. The government aided artists with its WPA program; Social Realist artists such as Ben Shahn and Philip Evergood appeared; along with Regionalist painters such as Edward Hopper, Thomas Hart Benton and Grant Wood; and abstractionists Charles Demuth and Stuart Davis.[153]

During the forties Hills' America was informed by the Abstract Expressionism of Jackson Pollock and Wilhelm de Kooning; the Realism of Andrew Wyeth and

Norman Rockwell; and the music of Billie Holiday, Louis Armstrong, Ella Fitzgerald, Bernie Goodman and Hank Williams.[154]

Meanwhile the fifties saw the polarization of America and its capitalism versus the Soviet Union and Communism; and the emigration of writers and artists from Europe, especially Germany, who were fleeing Naziism, to America's New York City, making of it an impressive new art capital.[155] Franz Kline, Pollock and his Action Painting and de Kooning and his Color Field painting continued in popularity with art innovators.[156] That Hills' pastels continued to enjoy an uninterrupted popularity throughout the approximately 32 years of their production, from the 1920s until her death in 1952, is surely a tribute to her tenacity and talent.

PERFECT PASTELS: ART HISTORICAL TRADITIONS

America's pastel art tradition began in an earlier time. As is true of the history of American miniatures, the history of American pastels began during the Colonial era. The first professional artist in America was a career woman who like Hills supported her family through the sale of her pictorial talents as equally a pastelist and portraitist.[157] This was, of course, Henrietta Johnston. Moreover, though, the history of pastels began in Colonial America predominantly though not exclusively as the artisan prerogative of men, until the late Victorian era when the budding of long-simmering feminism burgeoned into new career patterns for women, culminating in the flourishing of *their* artistic development. Hills and her peers well-exemplify this phenomenon. Still, the American tradition of pastels which Hills exemplified and developed to the highest popular level during her own era, differs from that of her Colonial predecessor most significantly in the area of iconography. While Johnston combined portraiture and pastels into a single expression, for Hills they were distinct endeavors. Hills' miniatures reveal sensitive portraits of men and women, while her pastels are equally proficient portraits of flowers.

The history of the use of pastels[158] in American art is a tradition which though conceived of early, struggled to reign with a steadily tempered hand, rather progressing intermittently, touting the efforts of such noteworthy painters as Copley, Trumbell, and Vanderlyn. Many artists were first of all painters; and secondarily, pastelists. Still, the nature of the use of pastel, especially relative to contemporaneous developments in such other graphic arts as watercolor, charcoal, engraving, and painting inform us of general artistic values operative throughout the various systems of aesthetics available to artists throughout the country, at any particular time. In addition, the history of pastels provides more specific insights into the changing visages of American art's notion of light and luminism, draftsmanship and abstraction, and later related practices affecting both public and private acceptance of Impressionism. And the subset of influences as converge within each group (social, literary, artistic) form signs of the underlying tripartite connection pictorialized by Hills' flower pastels: of the American Naturalism of her flower pastels; the Romantic Lyricism of the English Romantic poets; the stylistic discoveries in English and French Impressionism. It is this successful merger of American, French and English conventions visualized and proselytized which make of Hills' *oeuvre* overall an unmistakably magical innovation of aesthetics, and of each pastel an enduring, timeless, American icon.

American art, overall, plays host to nearly fifty primary and secondary pastelists, the latter being often first and foremost prominent painters. American pastelists may be grouped among the standard, categorical demarcations progressing from limner, folk, romantic, neoclassical, realist and Impressionist to surrealist. The register includes: Colonial artists, Henrietta Johnston, Joseph Blackburn, John Singleton Copley, William Dunlap, Benjamin West; Neoclassical portrait pastelist, John Vanderlyn; Naturalists John J. Audobon and William Morris Hunt; Hudson River School landscapist Thomas Doughty; Eastman Johnson, Thomas Eakins, Winslow Homer; Barbizon tonalist landscape pastelists including George Inness; the Romantic pastelists including Elihu Veddar; turn-of-the-century patriot and ex-patriot pastelists James Abbott McNeil Whistler, Mary Cassatt; Frank Duveneck, John LaFarge, William Merritt Chase; Impressionists Childe Hassam, J. Alden Weir; Tonalist Thomas Dewey, J. Carroll Beckwith; New York Realists (the Eight) inclusive of Robert Henri; Everett Shinn, Jerome Meyers; Precisionists Frank Stella; Biomorphic Abstractionist Georgia O'Keefe and Modernists William de Kooning, Wayne Thiebaud and Robert Blume.[159]

When miniature portraits reigned customary, painter, Henrietta Johnston was first to specialize in pastel portraits. Produced in the spirit of economic necessity, Johnston's pastel portraits adhered to the wide-eyed, frontal, three-quarter length formula of presentation derivative of the English portrait style as transmitted to America through Kneller's engravings which hinted at Baroque inspiration.

Colonial artist, John Smibert, promoted pastels in an era when they were routinely relegated to such commercial uses as landscape design, surveys, and architectural drawings. The English émigré, Joseph Blackburn, produced pastels and John Singleton Copley, renowned as "the first American draftsman in pastel", created influential pastels employing techniques presumed to have been learned from French drawing *livres*.[160]

Like Hills, some American artists, William Dunlap (*"Portrait of George Washington"*) designed both miniatures on ivory and pastel portraits. Inspired by the Neoclassical style, John Vanderlyn contributed the novelty of pastels drawn on various colored papers; while Naturalist John Audubon carried the torch of the artist-explorer, illustratively recording the science of bird species. Figural traditions of realist genre were continued by John Caleb Bingham, William Sydney Mount, Eastman Johnson, Thomas Eakins and Winslow Homer. Idiosyncratically, American landscapist William Morris Hunt infused his pastels with Barbizon moods and tones indicative of the pastel, monotone landscapes inspired not by English but rather such French sources as Francois Millet.[161] Meanwhile, Romantic pastelists searched their inner psyche and sublime nature for images with which to imbue their moody, pastel dreams, after the manner of the Impressionist novel, its fluctuating world, comprehensible only as an individually experienced array of spontaneous emotions cloaked in the guise of linear events, all prior to the advent of the optically inspired, scientific sensations of pictorial Impressionism.[162]

Regardless of categorical orientation, the universal appeal of the medium to all pastelists, the lure of pastels, involves the surrender to the general appeal of the medium as is rooted in several factors. These dimensions include: portability, for sketching interior scenes as well as those out-of-doors; in preference to oils, a comparative economy of means and lesser cost of production relative to size; greater potential for facile and rapid execution of images; a certain sumptuous facility of handling akin to dry oils; descriptive capabilities of stroke and accessibility to an impressive range of colors suitable to various purposes including those descriptive ends of the local colors of sense as associated with classic, Colonial considerations of objective and scientific fact. In addition, there were the suggestive possibilities of mystical tertiary colors characteristic of emotive sensibility as of the Barbizon and Symbolist artists' preoccupation with the interior psyche and subjective feelings. Then, there existed, of course, the vibrantly visual hues of abstract sensation associated with Impressionism.

Alluring also was the freedom pastels permitted for experimentation with different colored grounds, in combination with other media such as pencil, or ink, or paint; and an ability to create flattened decorative abstractions prior to Impressionism and later Modernist developments. Inherent in pastels are important Impressionist qualities. These include: opacity and hence flatness; unmodelled abstraction with broader lines, as yields a less volumetric effect analogous to flattened bits of prismatically colored form composed of the reflections of a certain type of light, in all events culminating in an object conducive to evocation of that significant aesthetic response. More than the conscious manner in which Hills uses pastels or the deliberate clouding of artistic vision by intervention of either the effects of memory or the veil of atmosphere, Hills' pastels have about them the aura of fluid perfection, whose ancestry heralds both Naturalism and Impressionism.

If, within the vernacular of Hills' floral pastels, Naturalism comprises the content of the forms Hills raises to symbolic heights; duality and evolution embody the hallmarks of her style. The art of Laura Coombs Hills, particularly her late pastels, displays overtones of French Impressionist values upon which critics of the time would have focused as they sought to explain Hills' art in terms of issues of form, light, and formalism, anticipatory to later twentieth century American art.

The emergence of Hills' flower pastels occurred in the wake of three important events. First, was the mid-nineteenth century French Objective Naturalist assertion, posited in the spirit of a reaction against Neoclassical aesthetic standards of the French Academy, which held that Nature was a sufficient cause, presented by itself, and in the absence of historical, mythical or allegorical iconography - a topical choice now valid for artists to embrace - and the subsequent legitimizing impact of this on the development of French Impressionist landscape and nature iconography. This was a significant change in nineteenth century Aesthetics.

Thus, one of the evolutionary accomplishments pastels share with watercolors is their kindred ability to ascend to levels higher than other decorative arts; both media's independent works each being worthy of a *bona fide* place of honor upon the hallowed walls of prestigious galleries; leaving behind their discarded identities as mere preliminary studies, amusing dalliances, or private meditations. Hills' pastels were not considered preliminary works. Hills' beautiful floral pastels were considered finished creations worthy of being hung not only on her patrons' walls, but on those of prestigious galleries and museums; thus, advancing the complete acceptance of pastels.

Second, were the innovations of nineteenth century color theorists such as Michel Eugene Chevreul (whose impact will be considered in the following section titled "Aesthetic Lyricism: Color Sensations; Color Harmonies")

And third, there was the influence of the preexisting tradition of floral pastels already practiced by Impressionist and post-Impressionist artists. Aiding general evolutionary trends are those specific to Hills' own life and times: her ties to Regionalist culture, the influence of her early teachers particularly Helen Mary Knowlton; early orientations acquired at Boston area educational institutions such as The Cowles School; New York lessons learned from renowned painter, pastelist, and educator William Merritt Chase; and insights garnered of expatriates abroad, inherent in Whistler's abstractions and Symbolist color harmony; the decorative abstraction of Sargent's watercolors; and Hills' own personal experiments.

To be considered a practitioner of French Impressionism working in America, that is an American Impressionist; Hills would have created in concert with an ethos, which paraphrased, advocates: a sense if not the fact of the dissolution of form into small, optical sensations as are abstract blocks of broad spectral color, broken color, and optical color mixing; gleaned from a highly keyed palette. These formalist concerns would be applied to out-of-door scenes of natural landscapes, images of enchanting women, actively engaged, portraits, flowers, or amenable cultural scenes of the enjoyable *bourgeoisie* life, captured from a unique perspective, perhaps as if in a downward glance from an upper story balcony. Inherent within would reside adherence to Objective Naturalist philosophy, a reaction against Neoclassicism and Romanticism, alignment with the new religion of agnosticism: the "Cult of Nature"; and an interest in light, especially bright daylight, and the changing meteorological conditions of its existence. Yet Hills creates no scenes of city boulevards, no repetitive subject series distinguished by alterations in light or season, no lovely ladies drinking tea in a garden setting, bathers on the beach, or ships anchored in color drenched harbors. Rather, she preferred, almost exclusively, pastel renderings of flower still-lifes.

Moreover, the iconography of Hills' oeuvre tends toward American choices, making of her an American Impressionist, an artist working in the Impressionist manner as applied to American iconography. In the environs of Boston, Hills may have identified more closely with the prevailing demographics, which were still predominantly English rather than French; while knowledge acquired through various teachers and influences brought to bear upon *their* experiences helped to define the various elements of her Impressionistic style - her line, form, and light.

Miss Jane Andrews was Laura Coombs Hills' first teacher, and though little is known of her guiding principles we may assume that since the sketching of pussy willows in a tumbler was one of Hills' first creations prompting such instruction; as an early student, a key issue, one which will resurface in her art, may have centered upon developing the empirical, naturalistic and decorative sides of Hills' sense of linearity. If little else, surely, encouragement would have been the order of the day.

Helen Mary Knowlton (1831-1918) may have presented the aspiring artist with an educational experience meaningful on several levels. It is perhaps because of Knowlton's background and potential points of influence, that Hills' artistic identity began to evolve, for Knowlton was, in part, what Hills would become. Both women would spend their lives as fellow, native New Englanders: Knowlton being born in Littleton, residing all her life in Needham; while Hills lived in Newburyport. Both would remain single and childless, preferring a life devoted to siblings and Art. Both would spend a significant amount of days professionally engaged within the graphics industry: Knowlton and her sisters as editors and publishers of their late father's newspaper, the Worcester Palladium; though Hills was less literarily inspired than Knowlton, who as well found herself penning thoughts for other newspapers including the Boston Post. Always Knowlton wrote of Art: "Talks on Art by William Morris Hunt", (1879), "Hints for Pupils in Drawings and Paintings" (1879). In addition, she painted Hunt's portrait[163], and it is here that personalities and aesthetics begin to intertwine for beyond publishing, and her own educational experiences in Boston, Philadelphia and London, which provided her with an orientation iconographically geared toward charcoal sketches, landscapes, and oil portraits, "the first medium being the most effective, there were French motifs: The Boston Museum of Fine Arts owns her *"Haystacks;"*[164] a subject familiar to Impressionists. Knowlton herself was influenced by the art of Hunt, Frank Duveneck, James Abbott McNeil Whistler, and William Merritt Chase. The *pleinairisme* of Duveneck and Chase may well have subtly infiltrated the art of Laura Coombs Hills through the respective intervention of Knowlton and her interest in Duveneck and Chase, the latter of whom, presumably, taught Hills herself the intricacies of pastel's light, line and form at New York's Art Students League.

The work of another native New Englander, born in Lowell, Massachusetts, an expatriot American residing in England, may similarly have served as inspiration. Beyond Whistler's[165] various roles as: mercurial herald of pastel art as President of the Society of British Artists, which formed the basic model for the Society of American Painters in Pastel; his creation of innumerable pastels; his travels to Venice; his effect upon American artists working in Italy; and association with the New English Art Club, is the *pleinairisme* evident in hundreds of his own pastels, many of which were exhibited in New York galleries, being as well known to artists here as to those abroad. In color, if more so in light, what Whistler's supporters shared was the pleinairist de-emphasis of detail as favored a generalized essence of form. This was accomplished partly through the eschewal of volumetric modeling as traditionally arises in the shadows with confluent, sequential gradations of tone; and partly through the application of brilliant bits of unadulterated color direct from the pastel's edge. What the English Symbolist, who so well touted the cause of Impressionist pastels, most eloquently shares with Hills, beyond *pleinairisme* beyond harmoniously constructed images, is a symphonic sumptuous color derivative of English lyricism and French Impressionism.

Hills' late pastels are increasingly diffuse, their pleinairiste white highlights evident upon the rims of petals and entire blossoms in clearly rendered sketches, broadly articulated in the wider, more abstract strokes Impressionists admired: more expressive, more two dimensionally decorative, and organized not after the fashion of a Dutch or American still-life, but as cropped magnified images, the envy of a bird's eye, filling the entire paper with only the primary element of blossoms. In her *"Larkspur, Peonies, and Canterbury Bells"* (purchased by the Boston Museum of Fine Art in 1926), Hills has merged Impressionist and Symbolist qualities to produce a harmony of abstraction, evocative of emotive color, each flower grouping: a choir of joyful brilliance.

Yet, ironically, amidst much art historical fanfare about the effects of color and more so light, its types and appearances: dissolved, diffused, prismatic, full- spectral, French, English, Tonalist, Glare Aesthetic, day, evening; in her typically unpretentious fashion, Hills herself may have admitted her light and its intense reflective power of color, to be wholly her own - attributing her success to Yankee ingenuity and the individual psyche. As with her miniatures, so too, perhaps with her pastels: not only was "her little finger her most valued tool", for enhancing the decorative blending of her increasingly abstract bits of color; but doubtless partially to accommodate extremely strong, yet near-sighted eyes, and part in the spirit of necessity as the mother of invention, the artist found that:

> It was "...the *electric light*...(which) made all the difference...It woke those lilies up, made them speak...The whole arrangement looked different under the combination of brilliant sunlight and artificial light."[166]

AESTHETIC LYRICISM: COLOR SENSATIONS, COLOR HARMONIES

"...around 1600,...Sir Isaac Newton revealed the true nature of color and devised the first of all color circles....According to Newton all colors were contained in white light. White light...was made up of bundles of rays of atoms which the prism could separate...Newton chose seven principal colors and allied them to ...the seven notes of the diatonic scale in music: red (note C), orange (note D), yellow (note E), green (note F), blue (note G), indigo (note A) and violet (note B)..."[167]

Or, as Faber Birren states: "Red colors are "loud" like the blare of a trumpet. Violin tones are like tints. The sound of the oboe is violet. Bass notes are brown, percussion notes are orange. All of color is thus human and seems to relate to all of life and all of sensation and experience in life."[168]

Remarkable in their resplendent use of hues, the floral pastels of Laura Coombs Hills are, each and all, beautiful, mellifluous choirs and symphonies of color, making of the artist America's Lyrical Impressionist.

As such, Hills continues the American tradition of Whitman's sentiments and practice of conferring majesty upon the mundane, the ordinary, the everyday. We recall that Whitman once tellingly wrote:

> I believe a leaf of grass is no less than the journeywork of the stars,
> ....And the cow crunching with depress'd head surpasses any statue,
> And a mouse is miracle enough to stagger sextillions of infidels [169]

For Hills, her fascination centered upon the apotheosis of native flowers growing in her own back yard in Newburyport, Massachusetts. These portraits of flowers became the undeclared agrarian icons of America's natural bounty. They were offered up to patrons as escapist, apolitical visions of an idyllic, natural world quickly fading in a country in the throes of Modernism in art and industrialization in society.

If held in the balance by the previous era's, mid-nineteenth century American Naturalism as it sprang from the philosophical shoulders of English Natural Law's property rights of civil society, melding and burgeoning in its association with Jeffersonian agrarianism and Jacksonian democracy; the dual lure of science and the wilderness surely beckoned finding a common voice as well in the spoken, written line. The poetry of Whitman best synopsizes the spirit of these sentiments. All of nature from the simplest forms was deemed beautiful, worthy, God-inspired, thus awe-evoking and hence iconographically desirable. The naked object of nature by the very simplicity of its objective form: eloquent, empirically realistic, democratically observable, stood elevated to its grandest apotheosis as this era begat the artistic veneration of species. Though in a different medium, it was still an iconographic tradition adopted by Hills.

And in keeping with her Time's newly burgeoning interest in publications relating to the psychology of color, in business, marketing, interior design, and psychiatric therapy, Hills' floral pastels became as well the psychological proponents of joy and vibrant life. Although admittedly culturally sensitive, colors and the color wheel/ chart had already acquired various meanings for America's art.

No longer subscribing to the notion of Aristotle that: "Simple colors are the proper colors of the elements, i.e. of fire, air, water and earth"[170] or Leonardo da Vinci's view that the proper roster of colors included: "...yellow for the earth, green for water, blue for air, red for fire, and black for total darkness"[171]; J. C. Le Blon had (in 1731) discovered the primary nature of red, yellow and blue in pigment mixture...This was the beginning of the red, yellow, blue theory.[172] In 1766, Morris Harris had published the first color chart in full hues featuring the red, yellow, blue theory. Harris also spoke of prismatic or primitive colors (red, yellow, blue), mediate colors (orange, green, and purple), and compound colors which artists today refer to as tertiaries that included olive (orange plus green), slate (green plus purple), and brown or russet (purple plus orange).[173] So by 1772 this theory was accepted, with proponents including Philipp Otto Runge and Johann Wolfgang von Goethe[174]; and the nineteenth century French color theorist, Michel Eugene Chevreul, whose work influenced the French Impressionists.

During the America of Hills' early life, Louis Prang, Milton Bradley, Arthur Pope, and Herbert E. Ives contributed significantly to contemporaneous art education by acting as author-proponents of the red, yellow, blue theory (also spoken of as the Brewsterian theory[175]); even though there existed prior to this, several opposing theories of color. Some of those theories included: the red, green, blue combination proposed by Wilhelm von Bezold of Munich in his book *The Theory of Color* (published in England in 1876 by Louis Prang of Boston); and Michel Jacobs' 1923 book *The Art of Color* whose principles of color harmony were based on the red, green, violet primaries.[176] And there was, of course, Albert Munsell's green, vermillion and purple blue system; Wilhelm Otswald's color chart, influenced by Ewald Hering's work and comprised of red, yellow, sea green, and blue primaries, with intermediaries of orange, leaf-green, turquoise, and purple. And there was the concept of the psychologist in which red, yellow, green, and blue are primary; a system to which Ewald Hering subscribed around 1870, "which has since been fully accepted by psychologists."[177]

Today, the red, yellow, blue color wheel is generally the most prevalent, along with the following psychological meanings. Red conjured passion, love, anger. Orange fostered energy, happiness and vitality. Yellow connoted happiness, hope, deceit. While green was associated with new beginnings, abundance and nature; and blue with calmness, responsibility, and sadness. Purple signaled creativity, royalty and wealth; while black foretold mystery, elegance, evil; and gray heralded moodiness, and conservative formality. White triggered associations with purity, cleanliness and virtue; and cream or ivory - calmness, elegance and purity. Lastly, beige was touted as the conservative, pious, dull color; while brown meant associations with wholesomeness, dependability and nature.[178]

Hills continues the reign, in New England, of a type of Impressionism associated with Boston artists, which retains as one of its earmarks, the prevailing identification of form rather than its total dissolution into blocks of bright, broken colors. Hills' flowers are always as easily identifiable empirically as those images of natural species produced by the earlier, Colonial artists - America's journalist-recorders, such as William Bartram.[179]

Moreover, while Hills' work combines a sense of American Empiricism plus New England Regionalism, it also exhibits the remnants of tenets of French Impressionism - especially ideas on color and design as espoused by Michel Eugene Chevreul, whose famous book, *The Principles of Harmony and Contrast of Colors and their Application to the Arts*, was published in 1839 by Hills' employer, Louis Prang Chromolithographers of Boston, Massachusetts.

In her informative, catalogue article on Hills titled "Breaking the Accepted Rules of Color", Sandra B. Lepore recounts the story of the interaction which produced her controversial title.

> "Frank Bayley of the Copley Gallery in Boston "accused her [Hills] of committing everything short of murder in breaking the accepted rules of color." Her [Hills'] response was, "I don't know about the rules, I was experimenting. Use of color depends so much upon balance, shape and manipulation."[180]

If Bayley had in mind the formal color theory of the old French Academies which espoused such ideals as: bright colours should be used sparingly; colour should be naturalistic; the paint surface should be smooth with no trace of brushstrokes; iconography should be intellectual and rational, such as with historical or biblical subjects; content should include a moral message; and idealized rather than overly realistic forms with close attention to detail; realistic modeling, shading and perspective; should be preferred;[181] or the eighteenth century advice of Edmund Burke[182] presented in an earlier chapter of this book, who advocated as most beautiful the softer colors of nature - the paler blues, and gentler greens; then Bayley would have been correct in stating that Hills broke the accepted rules of color.

But, as Faber Birren notes, "the Impressionists were devout students of color."[183] And Hills was an Impressionist and, hence, subscribed to many, although not all, of their practices. Thus, Hills did not break the accepted rules of color - she was simply adhering to her own era's accepted rules of color, following a newer methodology - one centered around Impressionist principles adopted from Chevreul and the Brewsterian color wheel - and, as well, her own guiding principles. Hills' innovative color theory doubtless evolved as forged from several sources including: her early teachers such as Knowlton, and later Chase at the New York Art Students' League; her employment experiences as a designer at Prang Chromolithographers; her "innate preference for enhanced local color"; Chevreulian color theory associated with earlier French Impressionists; and, of course, her own experiments.

Some of her earliest exhibited works (which were landscapes) show the effects of Barbizon painters and Knowlton's influence[184] in their overall color scheme. Later, Hills' earliest flower pastels would present as Impressionist artifacts, perhaps reflecting her brief but propitious time spent at New York's Art Students' League and the influence of Chase. Generally considered, though, Hills adopted the following Impressionist attributes and practices: a color theory based predominantly upon the Brewsterian[185] notation commonly known as the proponent of the Red, Yellow, Blue primary color circle; and secondarily, the printer's notation[186] of the Magenta, Yellow and Cyan color wheel so that she had at her disposal primary, secondary or intermediate, and tertiary colours. In addition, identifiable brushstrokes; the use of broken color and a limited palette of pure color; "rejection of illusionism; the elevation of contemporary subjects; the emphasis on the act of painting";[187] the bird's-eye perspective; important principles of Chevreulian color theory such as those centered upon color harmonies (adjacent and analogous); and working in the studio and "painting" *en plein aire* were all included in the tenor of the times of Hills' Impressionism.

Of course Hills had her own homegrown principles to follow such as those associated with her innovative use of the electric light to increase illumination on her floral bouquets; the use of her favorite color combinations such as adjacent and analogous harmonies; and her harmonies of complementary contrasting colors, and, in other pastels, her use of local color and her virtual eschewal of brown, gray, and black.

Many of Hills' practices are in keeping with the theories of Chevreul. He proposed ten general principles including those of: 1) volume; 2) form; 3) stability; 4) colour; 5) variety; 6) symmetry; 7) repetition; 8) general harmony; 9) fitness of the object for its destination; and 10) the principle of distinct view.[188] Many of Chevreul's general ideas are relatively straightforward; yet his specific ideas centered upon color harmony were altogether innovative and previously not addressed by artists and theorists. Chevreul even had recommendations applicable to landscape gardeners:

> "...the gardener should so employ his art that every plant intended
> to be seen in a state of isolation be large and beautiful, that it receives
> the light equally on every part."[189]

Perusal of Hills' flower pastels reveals her adherence to several other of Chevreul's principles, beyond his notations on color harmony. For example, Hills and Chevreul concurred on the following:

> "If the principle of variety recommends itself because it is contrary to
> monotony, it should be carefully restrained in its applications, because
> even without falling into confusion, effects may be produced far less
> agreeable than if they had been more simple."[190]

> "The repetition of an object, or a series of objects, produces greater
> pleasure than the sight of a single object, or of a single series."[191]

> "[General] Harmony is established between different objects by
> means of an analogy of size, of form, and of colour; by means of
> symmetrical position; and lastly, by means of repetition of the same
> form, of the same colour, or of the same object, or even of objects very
> analogous, if they are not identical."[192]

> And, finally..."It is necessary for every work of art to satisfy the
> principle of distinct view, by which all the parts of a whole intended to
> be exhibited, should present themselves without confusion and in the
> simplest manner."[193]

In addition, Chevreul set forth several principles for the harmony of color: 1) the harmony of adjacent (analogous) colors; 2) the harmony of opposite colors; 3) the harmony of split complements; 4) the harmony of triads; and 5) the harmony of a dominant tone. His findings "greatly influenced and inspired the Impressionist and Neo-Impressionist painters of France during the latter part of the nineteenth century."[194] Moreover, "...studies in the field of psychology have verified the observation of Chevreul that colors look best (a) when they are closely related or analogous or (b) when they are complementary or in strong contrast."[195]

Regarding the harmony of adjacent (analogous) colors, these colors are those located next to each other on the color circle. Analogous colors have an emotional quality, for they favor the warm or cool side of the spectrum.[196] With analogous color schemes, "effects are generally best when the key hue is a primary (red, yellow, blue) or a secondary (orange, green, violet)."[197] Thus, for example, a good color scheme would be: Blue with blue-green and blue-violet; Orange with red-orange and yellow orange; and so forth, such that the simple primary or secondary is supported and enhanced by two intermediate colors that reflect its character and lie on either side of it on the color circle."[198]

Regarding the harmony of opposites, Chevreul wrote: "The contrast of the most opposite colors is most agreeable...The complementary assortment is superior to every other."[199] Thus, on the color circle, opposites would be as follows: Red and green; Red-orange and blue-green; Orange and blue; Yellow-orange and blue-violet; Yellow and violet; and Yellow-green and red-violet.[200] The significance of this is that in these types of combinations, the two chosen, complementary colors each heighten the effect of the other. In addition, Chevreul's rule of simultaneous contrast occurs: that is, if two colors are close together in proximity, each will take on the hue of the complement of the adjacent color.[201]

According to Chevreul, a more advanced contrast is gained by the use of "split complements". "Here a key color is combined with the two hues that lie next to its exact opposite."[202] Examples of this phenomena include: blue-violet with orange and yellow; red with yellow-green and blue-green; blue-green with red and orange. Faber Birren states that there is more variety and beauty with the split complements than with the direct opposites alone.[203]

The harmony of the four triad possibilities include: 1) red, yellow, blue (the primaries); 2) orange, green, violet (the secondaries); 3) the intermediates - red-orange, yellow-green, and blue-violet; and 4) the intermediates - yellow-orange, blue-green, and red violet.[204]

Finally, there exists according to Chevreul, the harmony of a dominant tint. (Hills would have been more apt to use this in her miniatures than her pastels.) The significance of a tint is that it will effectively draw a group of colors together by introducing an all-pervasive tone.[205] This was a phenomenon which particularly interested the Impressionists since: "The colors of nature (and those fashioned by man) are commonly seen under tinted light that varies from the pink and orange of early dawn, to the yellow of sunlight, to the blue of sky light. Distance may be enveloped in grayish or purplish mist."[206] Or as Hills advocated - the supplementary use of an electric light to "wake up" the colors of her floral arrangements.

Hill's floral arrangements exhibited two distinct motifs. The first presented a horizontal hint of a table, with usually a round or curvy vase or bowl sitting atop the table, in front of some form of draped tapestry fabric. The second image was composed as a true French Impressionist artist might do: filling the entire canvas, looking down from a bird's eye view on an appropriately truncated arrangement of flowers with long stems.

Her favorite color combinations were of both the complementary type and the analogous or adjacent formula. For example, *The Little Yellow Pot* is filled with orange, gold, yellow and pale coral flowers, arranged in an orange bowl resting in front of blue drapery. A similar composition is Hill's *Yellow Pansies in a Bowl* which also forms a complementary color pattern of bright yellow flowers against a deep blue-violet background. In another pairing of complementaries, *Hollyhocks*, long stalks of bright red blossoms stand out against a hunter and pale green horticultural background.

As an alternative color scheme, Hills often employed an analogous or adjacent formula as is found in her *Calendulas* which reveal several different orange toned flowers against a deep orange drapery. In her *White Blossoms* she reveals another favorite pairing of adjacent colors in her blue-green and blue violet shades balanced against a tapestry of emerald and indigo. But, of course, her favorite pastel hues centered around the violet-purple tones, which pastels were unavailable in this country, but available and purchased in Europe by Hills at the art establishment of Henri Roche. Perhaps one of her most renowned pieces, purchased early on by the Boston Museum of Fine Arts, is an *a propos* example of her color preferences: and that would be her *Larkspur, Peonies and Canterbury Bells*.

Moreover, Hills might have agreed that "the science of color is highly personal and psychological; and that the science of color must...be regarded as essentially a mental science."[207] Or as Birren states in his book *The History of Color in Painting*: "Beauty (or ugliness) is not out *there* in man's environment, but *here* within man's brain. Where formerly some artists strove to find laws in nature, now one may be sure that such laws, if they exist at all, lie within the psyche of man....The perception of color - including feeling and emotion - is the property of human consciousness."[208]

The Critics

"Laura Coombs Hills

THOSE artists are rare who leave a dual mark upon their time, excelling in more than one medium. Laura Coombs Hills, of Boston, who is having an exhibition at the Ferargil Gallery, has performed this difficult feat. Her work as a miniaturist is well remembered, fine in color and marked by uncommon freedom in style, the work of a true painter. In more recent years her activity in the field of miniature has ceased and she has given herself, instead, to the painting of flower pieces in pastel. About thirty of them appear in the present exhibition, and they make an astonishing effect. Astonishing because, after working so long within the inexorable restrictions of the miniature, Miss Hills strikes out with a boldness, a force, a brilliance of color which give to her flower studies an extraordinarily sumptuous character. And her elan, her vigor in attack, is accompanied by great sureness of hand. She continues to be the authoritative craftsman, handling her technique with a confident ease that is by itself delightful to observe.

It serves her well in the manipulation of many keys, in the blaze of color captured in the *"Tulips"* or in the more subdued note of *"The Hurricane"*, wherein the flowers beaten by the storm are painted with a winning delicacy. At one moment she puts forth all her strength, as in the *"Peonies and Glass"*, and at another she is content to be merely exquisite, as in the *"Daffodils"* or the *"Yellow Pansies"*. When she formalizes her subject she is not at her best. Witness the rather stiff *"Garland of Roses"*, but that pastel denotes the only departure from her wonted distaste for convention. Everything else in the show testifies to the free manner in which she presents flowers, "in their natural" setting, distilling their essence but arranging them with a certain energy, and finally, with a distinctive touch. In taking leave of this exceptional exhibition, I must point out also the skillful painting of subsidiary motives, such as the basket in the *"Flowers and Shadows"*. It is one more evidence of the technician supporting the clairvoyant interpreter."[209]

United Press, 1940.

"...Laura Coombs Hills' glowing *"Zinnias and Copper"* and other flower compositions highlight the pastel group."[210]

Sunday Post, undated.

"Here finally are the glowing flower pastels of Laura Coombs Hills. No one has ever equaled her in this, and, though past 80 now, she is still without peer."[211]

United Press reviewing Post article.

"...The passage of time, especially nowadays, changes more things than we like to realize, but the exquisite delicacy, fresh coloring, and loving observation of Miss Hills' flower pastels remains unaltered. At 83, her hand is steady, her eye as true and her respect for her craft as unwavering as they have always been and anyone who still considers age a matter of years rather than of the spirit should visit these pictures, all of which with the exception of three or four have been done within the past few months.

So dear and fresh are the tints in the pictures that you feel they must have been painted under the open sky, that they have wandered indoors by mistake and lingered briefly on the walls of the gallery as sunlight strikes through clear glass. Even the texture of the petals is marvelously conveyed: the pansies have an exquisite velvety touch; the pond lilies their unmistakable crisp firmness, the Van Fleet roses are translucent, the peonies fresh and sturdy, the sunflowers glow with an inner light, the apple and blossoms hold delicate flush of pink in their tiny cups and the zinnias and delphiniums in the midsummer glory fairly radiate stored-up sunshine.

No less lively than the flowers themselves are the vases and backgrounds. Miss Hills has a wonderful gift with materials of a soft delicate color, her roses and tulips and pansies standout marvelously against green and yellow iridescence, or she will make the unique and successful experiment of setting pinkish red tulips and white freesias against a reddish pink background that harmonizes but does not blend. Her vases may be clear glass, gold white, blue or neutral tinted pottery, but they all have a peculiar fitness. Out of the present exhibition of 28 pastels, each beholder will have to pick his favorite: there are several types of roses, large and small, sunflowers, lilies, irises, exquisite primroses, pansies, zinnias, and pond lilies, peonies, delphiniums, and pinks, all lovely, all fresh and alive."[212]

United Press Review of
Annual GBA Exhibition,
March 29, 1943.

"...An exhibition of flowers in pastel by Laura Coombs Hills at the age of 84 indicates that the creative life of an artist goes far beyond the span of usefulness achieved by most business folk. Miss Hills' work at the Guild of Boston Artists contains all the freshness of her earlier specimens and is even more daring, from the point of view of the colorist, than it was fifty years ago. Here is indeed a remarkable record, and an inspiration to younger artists."[213]

Boston Herald, December 1944

"...The Guild of Boston Artists is now presenting the annual and always pleasantly anticipated exhibition of pastels of flowers by Laura Coombs Hills, an artist whose love for subjects and skill in depicting them does not falter with the years. It is a pleasure and a refreshment to visit her shows this year no less than in previous seasons.

There are 29 pictures in the big gallery at the Guild of which *"White Petunias"* and *"Harrison Roses"* have been lent for the occasion, and the other 27 of which appear to be new. It is interesting this year Miss Hills has not kept entirely to the soft, delicate hues that usually predominate in her exhibits, but has painted a number of studies such as *"Macaw"* showing a bright blue vase of orange flowers against an equally bright blue scarf, the whole thing set against an orange-yellow ground; *"Zinnias"* showing red, yellow and pink blossoms against a pink-red ground; and *"Pottery from Peru"*, a curious little black figure against a background of sun-flowers.

Also by way of novelty there is a charming portrait of a young girl in white, entitled *"The May Queen"* in which the subject's dark hair is crowned with a wreath of spring flowers and flowers are grouped around her; and there is also an unusually formal grouping *"Garland of Roses"* showing pink roses arranged in a garland supported by three vases of classic design.

Of particular charm among the other paintings are *"White Against White"*, appleblossoms in a pale blue jar against an opalescent ground; *"Larkspur and White Iris"*, an exquisite study in soft blues and pale yellow; *"Petunias and Pewter"* a delicately lovely combination of pale pink, white and soft gray; *"Larkspur and Lilies"*, which speaks for itself; *"Spring Flowers"*, *"Harrison Roses"*, showing white roses in a beautiful copper bowl; and *"Yellow Roses"*.[214]

Boston Herald, December 5, 1943

"...Pastel portrayals of flowers by Laura Coombs Hills are to be seen currently at the Guild of Boston Artists, The Guild gallery looks festive and cheerful in this flowery profusion and in the next few weeks many a visitor will come to be refreshed by the exhilarating compositions.

Laura Coombs Hills has made miniatures and pastels for many years...The decades in which she has worked have seen many alternatives and innovations. But Miss Hills has carried on steadily and devotedly, making pictures in accordance with her own convictions.

Few artists have maintained her freshness and enthusiasm, few have been able to work over such a span of years without settling into conventions and cliches. Each new effort with Miss Hills is a fresh adventure, a new challenge, and invariably she has permitted the blossoms portrayed full authority as though it were her duty to record and objectify their special charms. Reared in the tenets of naturalism, she has always had her eye upon the model, and sought the typifying shape, texture, bearing and hue. An artist might fulfill those requisites and yet not achieve her vividness and distinctiveness.

In the Guild display are her most recent pastels, supplemented with earlier portraits. *"Flowering Crab"* reveals a clarity of definition in which she is especially skilled. She has set pink blossoms against a flaming vermilion. The backgrounds, are always carefully arranged for bold contrast or delicate enhancement. The containers, too, are thoughtfully chosen glass, metal, ceramic.

The flowers of Miss Hills appeal to the gardener, the lover of the outdoors. They are flowers that the artist has raised and handled. She knows their "personalities", when they have come from the florist, she says so in the title."[215]

United Press, 1940s

"Laura Coombs Hills Show

...At the Guild of Boston Artists recent pastels by Laura Coombs Hills are on exhibition. Miss Hills is the Dean of Flower Portraitists in New England. She is greatly admired and her drawings have gained countless admirers. In her long career as an artist, she has won many awards and mentions. She continues to work with noteworthy delicacy, grace and attentiveness. The flowers are portrayed with affection as well as understanding. They are set forth in the maximum of blossomy charm. She portrays them as though they had temperament, as though possessed with some distinctive quality of grace. They are clearly articulated and the textures are admirably reproduced.

Among outstanding pictures in the exhibition are *"English Primroses," "White Roses," "Van Fleets", "Shirley Poppies", "Larkspur and Lilies"* and *"Pink Dahlias"*. The last is a most luxuriant assemblage of blossoms in a warm light."[216]

American Art Annual, 1925

"Flower Painting Exhibit Attracts Enthusiasts by A.J. Philpott

....Flower painting in pastels by Laura Coombs Hills in Guild of Boston Artists, 162 Newbury Street, attracted attention...in art circles she is spoken of as "Queen of Flower Painters"...prior to that she was known as "Queen of Miniature Painters". Laura Coombs Hills has always been in a class by herself. She is 88 years of age and painting with the enthusiasm of a woman of 50. She has probably sold more paintings than any artist in the United States and is as popular as ever. She is a wonder! The 31 pastel paintings in the exhibition were done the past year. The curious thing: she took up flower painting as a sort of relaxation from miniature portraits. The skills in drawing and painting which she has developed in miniature painting distinguished her flower paintings from the beginning. When news of that first exhibition in the Doll and Richards Gallery got about in art circles something happened the like of which had probably never been known before in Boston. There was a crowd waiting at the doors every morning for the gallery to open, and the crowd continued until the gallery closed in the afternoon.

Nearly all the pictures were sold the first day. This sort of thing continued for years - until she was elected as a member of the Guild of Boston Artists. This present exhibition shows that her popularity has not waned. A Laura Coombs Hills picture is still considered an art treasure. Exhibition will continue to December 6.[217]

Boston Globe, November 23, 1947.

(The) joyous complex of her pastels are an extension of her delightful, graciously hospitable personality, punctuated by an inexhaustible sense of fun.[218]

Unknown paper.

SUMMARY

Throughout her long life and career, Laura Coombs Hills has been thought of primarily within the traditional context of an art historical perspective, as the remarkable creator of marvelous miniatures and perfect pastels. Yet, her overall contribution to American culture comprised so much more.

Although her first notable introduction to miniatures occurred on a trip abroad to England, art historically, her miniatures emerged out of the American miniature tradition. Having as her artistic ancestors the works of such notable figures as John Robinson (*Mrs. Pierre Hurtell*); Thomas Seir Cummings (*The Bracelet*; wife, Jane Cook); Anne Hall of Connecticut (*The Artist with Her Sister, Elizabeth Ward Hall and Master Henry Hall*); and Henrietta Johnston's portraits; Hills drew upon several aspects of the evolving traditions of these artists.

First and foremost, was the concentration on intellectual Sense or epistemological reality: what could be truly seen with the mind through the operation of the senses. The faces, the figures, and the accoutrements were of paramount significance. American miniatures were shrouded in the veil of verisimilitude. Faces and figures were to be faithfully rendered in accordance with physiognomy. Hills' critics confirm for us her mastery of this requisite skill. The critics praised her ability to capture the essence of, not only accurate, physical representation, but as well, the sitter's particular personality. On a broader level, this speaks to the parallel destinies of the American literary tradition's connection to biography and the art historical life of the miniature.

The focus on function, as it is tied to representations of personality and sentiment, forms another dynamic between the precursors to Hills' miniatures and her own. Those works which existed previously, especially the miniatures made during the American Civil War era, paraded personality, physiognomy and function hand-in -hand with sentiment and sensibility. And once again, we see the parallel destiny between literature and the arts in the persistence of romance. The function of both derivations of miniature portraits was that of a sentimental keepsake. Most often they were presented to a loved one as an aid to cherishing a romantic memory. As such, both types of miniatures embodied nothing short of treasured jewels.

Overall, the joyful, Whitmanesque sense of celebration of all things American, especially the country's men as well as its women, pervades the sense of preciousness which the critics so admired in Hills' miniatures of the male and female residents of New England's Newburyport, Massachusetts.

And, both Whitman's sense of dignity anchored in the everyday object and a similar sense of exuberant vitality is echoed as well in Hills' other portraits – those subjects selected from her very own garden at "The Goldfish" – which morphed into her pastel portraits of well-tended flowers. In this choice of iconography, Hills differed from her American ancestors, such as Henrietta Johnston, who was well known for her pastel portraits of people. And in another sense Hills differed from earlier prototypes in the wealth and richness of her sense of color sensations – for this exploration into optics is very much the inherent, innovative subject of her pastels.

Admiring Hills' floral pastels for the initial time, we readily notice her vibrant use of the inland and seaside hues of her hometown of Newburyport. And as well, we note the clarity of articulation and strength of individuality that the artist imparts to each everyday species – plebian or patrician – which she chooses to enliven with her democratic spirit of optimistic vitality.

Essentially, Hills' pastels are comprised of two distinct styles. The first one, conceived early on was followed continuously, the formula virtually unchanged through the years. With the second, later style, we see a faster evolution toward the newer ideas of enhanced Modernist and Impressionist abstraction. While the initial style presents as a basic iconographic formula derivative of Dutch, English, and early American conceptualization; the later style offers a more modern, Europeanized format.

The earlier floral still life pastel is composed of realistically, representationally correct vases overflowing with some specific types of New England flowers. The image is centrally positioned overall, poised atop a ground inferred to be a table top, though not specifically so delineated; all situated in front of a dramatically folded, luxurious fabric reminiscent of the sumptuous drapery backgrounds of Baroque English portraiture. The basic structural dimensions into which the canvas is divided consist of a lower ground constituting one fourth of the space, with all else being frontally presented as if seen at eye level. The smaller flowers: violets, roses, and pansies, prove most congenial to this arrangement.

The second, later style, progresses with greater fervor from the stylistic affinities of realistic Impressionism characteristic of Boston and its environs toward kinship with the work of Claude Monet ("Irises") before stopping short of Georgia O'Keefe's biomorphic abstraction. Such later trends move from the investigative enlargements of Realism toward innovation with the adoption of the French Impressionist bird's-eye view; later Impressionism's abstracted, decorative florals; the visually melodic incorporation inherent in overtones derivative of the color harmonies of Whistler;

the freer representational forms reminiscent of Monet's late flowers; and the refined, scrutinized individuation of species typical of organically vital Nature.

The climate conducive to the acceptance and reason for the popularity of Hills' pastels – the vibrant color harmonies paired with recognizable American species, would in other painters, constitute a formula warranting the label of "American Impressionist". Yet Hills' contributions and her place in Art are related to, yet extend beyond this general categorical distinction, as she carves out a niche all her own as "America's Lyrical Impressionist".

By continuing the pre-existing tradition of American pastels, Hills was a revivalist. By devising her own traditions associated with pastels, Hills was equally an innovator and a highly competent, technical artist. If not perhaps one of the best pastelists in American art, as she was considered by critics of her own time, then surely she places a close second behind a handful of practitioners in that medium.

Perhaps of primary significance is the fact that Hills assimilated aspects of American, English, and French traditions. Impressionism, Regionalism, and Naturalism were as important to her creative instincts in pastels, as ambient reflections of American and English poets of the nineteenth century were to her miniatures.

Further, Hills' oeuvre marks several important milestones exemplifying the best of American pastels. Their solitary subjects, portraits, here of flowers, address the legacy of Colonial Naturalism, its rebirth in the cultural concerns of the Victorian era as it fervently expressed its own interest in the legacies of the English "Cult of Nature" inspired as a reaction to industrialism, becoming inherently its symbol, and presaging the creation of America's own exemplars. These symbols, these floral pastels by Laura Coombs Hills, were quite appropriate to and popular with Americans who purchased them not only on the basis of inspiring aesthetics, but perhaps, if subconsciously, as nostalgic, idyllic symbols of America. Indeed, Hill's pastels were enormously popular with the art world that Boston's Blue Book subculture embraced – the conservative art world of Boston tradition.

Hills' pastels are unique in the confluent stream of influences for Hills merges the artistic bases of her American, pastelist predecessors of Colonial times with relatively newer French interests in optical sensations. Chevreulian color theory in particular graced Hills' pastels. Here Hills utilizes vibrant hues, not in an antagonistic manner as perhaps did other artists, but rather in an enlivening way. Colors that in others' hands might have clashed, in Hills' hands put forth an emboldened image that is nothing less than supremely captivating. And, upon this factor also, her contemporary critics commented enthusiastically. Indeed, in their singular concentration on the sensual qualities of prismatic, lyrical light and full spectral color, Hills' floral pastels mirror Impressionist issues related to light and color theory. Her pastels also reflect, perhaps to a lesser degree, the veil of Impressionistic dissolution and its relationship to both naturalism and representational abstraction on the process of artistic reaction, all finally culminating in that particular aesthetic response which these creations arouse within us.

As such, Hills' pastels became an important transmitter of a foreign aesthetic. These pastels merge Impressionistic concerns, especially those sensations of color and light, to produce an image of beauty drawn from nature, which is so pleasing to our senses that we not only imagine the flowers' tactile sensations, but almost as well, their very fragrance. Moreover, in their capacity to trigger an interior emotional and psychological response of pleasure, that is of sensory pleasure as opposed to the cognitive joy of familiar, intellectual recognition, Hills pastels are essentially sensual in spirit.

As such, they are close to the sentiments aroused by the shared values residing in the works of the English Romantic Lyric poets, American Transcendentalist poets, and the introspections of Naturalist and Impressionist writers. And, if Hills' role and contribution to advancing Impressionism in the United States is not one of primary leadership, that is, not prototypical; it was then certainly archetypal since her work achieves a new zenith of technical expertise amidst all practitioners as she creates quintessential conduits of culture and icons of taste consistent with the development of her own, stylistically innovative American Lyrical Impressionism.

As noted previously, Hills managed to achieve many milestones. Hills is a significant figure in the history of American art. Laura Coombs Hills' contributions to American culture entailed more than merely the creation of splendid, sumptuous miniatures and pastels. A highly competent technical artist, she became a revivalist in the world of American miniature traditions; an innovator of a unique, new American style of miniature; a promulgator, into the twentieth century, of nineteenth century *zeitqeist* associated with Walt Whitman's celebratory outlook for all things American – her men, her women, her bountiful Nature; a perpetuator of miniatures as sentimental keepsakes of romance (so prevalent during the American Civil War era); and a purveyor of the societally integrated, nineteenth century concept of the individual into her own, fractured twentieth century.

In the world of pastels, Hills was also a revivalist, a traditionalist, and an innovator. She was a forerunner in the twentieth century American revival of pastel art; the exemplar of an earlier, American art tradition of the art-journalist emphasizing empiricism; as well as a solicitor for their elevation to the rank of a *bona fide* art form as well-received and valuable as were paintings; a conduit for multiple cultural trends of American, French and English derivation, perhaps most importantly those centered around the transmission to the New England art scene of Chevreulian color theory and its bold and innovative emphasis on combinations of analogous and opposing color; and a foremost practitioner of an elegant art form. Hills was the creator of entirely new traditions in American art.

Perhaps most simply and appropriately, just as Lilian Westcott Hale may be thought of as America's Linear Impressionist because she uniquely used the verticality of line in an Impressionist manner applied to American iconography; Hills may be called America's Lyrical Impressionist because all of her works sing out in such mellifluous tones of color. Moreover, Hills successfully combined important aesthetic concerns of her own time, that is, various types of Impressionism with significant elements and types of literary lyricism, both American and English, into beautiful renderings of archetypical American subjects of great beauty and sensitive lyricism – of Sense, Sensibility and Sensation.

Appendixes

Appendixes

Known Works - Multi-Media
Known Works - Miniatures
Known Works - Floral Pastels
Awards, Medals, Honors and Prizes
Museum and Gallery Associations
Exhibition History
Index to Reproductions
Endnotes
Bibliography
About the Author

List of Known Works - Multi-Media

Architectural Designs for her home, 'The Goldfish'

Miniature Doll Costumes and Designs for Patricia
in the style of the 1860x including:
Lilliputian parasol
Authentic hoop skirt
Flannel petticoat
Silk stockings
Black satin slippers
White satin, lace-trimmed corsets
Hand-stitched gloves

Crayon and Pastel Portraits

Painted China

Designs for Needlepoint, Cross-stitch and Embroidery

Watercolor Landscapes

Silhouette Paper Portraits

Christmas Cards and Posters

Chromolithographs and Valentines for Louis Prang of Boston

Illustrations for Poems and Verses

China designs for the Merrimac Potters

Book illustrations for 'Flower Folk' by Anne M. Pratt.

Costume Design for 'The Snake'

Calendars, Cards and Posters

Costume Design for 'Every Boy'

Penciled, Illustrated Poetry

Organized,
Supervised,
Choreographed,
'The Pageant of the Year'
Mechanics Hall, Boston,
December 1882
for
The Woman's Industrial Union of Boston

Two oil paintings

St. Nicholas Illustration

Known Works by Laura Coombs Hills

Miniatures

A

Portrait of Catherine Arms

B

Mrs. B.

Mrs. Berenstrieff

Master Clement Bernheimer

Miss Marjorie Bernheimer

Mrs. Mayer S. Bernheimer

Mrs. Frederick Billings

Miss Francis Biddie

Billy

Persis Blair

Master John Blarney

The Black Hat

Mrs. Edwin St. Blashfield

The Black Mantle

The Blue Bandeau

The Bride

Miss Alice Brown

Annie Brown

Boy Blue

Butterfly

C

Miss C.

Calendules

Hannah Carey

Miss Agnes A. Childs (Sunshine)

Convalvulus Minor

Miss Bertha Coolidge (Mrs. Marshall Slade)

Mrs. Royal Crane

Master George Glover Crocker, 3rd.

Mary Creasy (Crecy)

D

Miss Madeline Davis

Mrs. Basil DeSelincourt (Anne Douglas Sedgewick)

Dorothy

Miss Katherine Dreier

E

Master John Edsall

Miss Mary Ellory

English Daisys and Forget-Me-Nots

Master Governor Ely, Jr.

June L. Everett

F

Mrs. John Cummings Fairchild

Fire Opal (Grace Nuttell)

The Flame Girl

The Flower Girl

Large Bowl of Flowers

Old Fashioned Flowers

G

Miss G.

An Irish Girl

Girl in Green

Girl with Violets

The Goldfish (Girl with Red Tresses)

Mrs. Edwin Farnhorn Green
Miss Ruth Graves
Miss Louis Graves
Miss Isabel da Costa Green

H

M. H.

Miss H.

Edward Everett Hale, 3rd.

Margaret Curzon Hale (Margie in White)

Miss Grace Hall

Mrs. Emmons Hanlin

Edith Harlon (2)

Arthur Harlow

Helen Harlow

Mr. (Robert?) Hartshorne

Mrs. Robert Hartshorne

'At Anne Hathaway's'

Mrs. Sidney Haywood (Beatrice Herford)

Master Pierre Hazard

'He'll Come Back to Marry Me'

Mrs. Elwood Hendrick

Hillside Iris

Miss Lizzie Bayley Hills (Sister)

Mr. Philip Knapp Hills (Father)

Mary Huse

I, J

A Little Jaz

K, L

A Lady of Quality

Lady with Violets (Mrs. J. Perkins)

Larkspur and Lilies

Laura

Master William Lusk

M

Master Valentine Evert Macy
Little Agnes MacIntosh
Marshes Near Newburyport
May Queen
Mildred (Miss Howells)
Master Donald Moffat
Mrs. Francis Morris
Miss Alice Josephine Morse
Mourning Cap
Mrs. Thomas Motley, Jr. (2)

N

Viola Nelson (The Pink Flower)
The Nymph

O

Old London House

P

Pink and Lavendar
Portraits (2)
Pansies
Peonies and Pyrethiums
Miss Georgiana Perkins
Mrs. Charles Platt
Carrie Pratt
Miss Elizabeth Pratt
Helen Pratt
May Pratt
Mrs. George Pratt.
Marjorie Prince
A Blonde Profile
Psyche

Q, R

Eleanor Pickering Randall

Ethel Reed

Mrs. Elizabeth Richardson

Henry Robbins

Master Philip James Roosevelt

Roses

Elizabeth Rutter

S

Saint Elizabeth

Self-Portrait

Self-Portrait in the Persian Manner

Miss Louis Scribner

Sister and Brother

Sleeping Girl

Snow Berries

Master Thomas Leffingwell Shipman

Miss Dorothy Little Stevens

Miss Laura Stevens

A Study

Study of a Blonde

Study of a Head

Study in Pink

Sunnyside Gladiolas

Elizabeth Swan

Mary Swan

T

Mrs. T.

U, V

Henry Vaughn

W

Mrs. Roger Warren
Miss Louise Wheeler
Miss Mary Louise Wheeler
Miss Dorothy Bass Whitney
White Music
Miss Natalie Wood

X

Y

The Yellow Scarf
Your Face Is Your Fortune
Youth

Z

Zinnias

Known Works of Laura Coombs Hills

Flower Pastels

A

Aunt's Garden

Apple Blossom

Apple Blossoms and Silver

B

Basket of Flowers

Basket of Fruit

Begonias

Blue and White

Bowl of Dahlias

Bowl of Flowers

Bowl of Mixed Flowers

Bowl of Zinnias

Breakfast

Briar Cliffe Rose

C

Calendulars and Stock

Calla Lillies

Cherokee Roses

Chinese Roses

Chinersis and Lilies

Crimson Roses

Crimson and Blue

March Marigolds
Mid-Day
Mixed Flowers
Mixed Flowers with Blue Background
Mixed Flowers with Gray Velvet
Mixed Flowers in White Jar
Morning

N

Nicatianas at Night
Night Blooming Cereus

O

Old Fashioned Flowers

P

Pale Pansies
Peonies and Glass
Peonies and Rocket
Pansies and Rose
Peonies
Petunias
Petunias (#2)
Petunias and Venetian Glass
Petunias and Gypsophilia
Petunias and Pewter
Phlox
Pink Appleblossoms
Pink Camellia
Pink Dahlias
Pink Flowers
Pink Roses and Larkspur
Pink and White Petunias
Pink and White Tulips
Pink and Yellow
Pink Roses with Buds

Pond Lilies
Poppies, Calendulas, and Euphobia
Poppies and Honey Pits
Pottery from Peru
Primroses

Q
The May Queen

R
The Rapture Rose
Red Geraniums
Red Lillies
The Red Tray
Red and White Camellias
Red, Yellow and Purple Zinnias
(on brown bowl on black-edged, gleaming table)
Rhododendrons
Roses (5)
Roses and Larkspur
Roses and Glass
Roses and Pink

S
Saligiglasis
Shirley Poppieis
Silver Moon Roses
Small Bowl of Zinnias
Snow Berries
Snowberries Against the Green
The Spanish Bowl
Spilled Poppies
Spring Flowers
Stock Petunias
Summer Amaryllis
Summer Flowers

Sun Flowers

Syringe

T

Talisman Roses

Tea Roses

Three Roses

Two Yellow Roses

Tulips

Tulips and Freezias

Tulips in Lamplight

U

V

Van Fleets

A Van Fleet Rose

W

West Cedar Street

White Against White

White Begonias

White and Blue

White Camellias

White Freezias

White and Gray

A White Chrysanthemum

White Jar of Flowers

White Jar of Yellow Roses

White Iris

White Petunias

White Petunias and Rocket

White Phlox and Sunshine

White Roses

White Roses in a Glass

White Petunias and Silver

White Phlox in Sunshine
A Winter Day

X

Y
Yellow Dahlias
Yellow Freezias
Yellow Jar
Yellow Nasturtiums
Yellow Pansies
Yellow Roses
Yellow Roses (#2)

Z
A Jar of Zinnias
A Bowl of Zinnias
Zinnias
Zinnias and Brass
Zinnias and Copper
Zinnias and Green
Zinnias and Marigolds
Zinnias and Silver
Zinnias and Stock

Honors, Medals and Awards

Sarah Orne Jewett	1893 Purchase	Sale of First Miniature
Art Interchange, New York	1895 Medal	
J. Eastman Chase, New York	1895; New orders - 27	First Solo Exhibition
New York, Unknown Gallery	1897 Silver Medal	Best Miniature
Art Amateur	1897 Silver Medal	The Flame Girl
Paris Exposition	1900 Medal	
Corcoran Gallery of Art	1901 Medal; $100 Prize	Grace Nuttel (Fire Opal)
Pan American Exposition, Buffalo	1901 Silver Medal	
Charlestown Exhibition	1902 Silver Medal	
Universal Exposition, St. Louis	1904 Gold Medal	
National Academy of Design	1906 Associate Status	
Pan American Art Exposition	1915 Medal of Honor	
Pennsylvania Academy of Miniature Painters	1916 First Award of Honor	
Pennsylvania Academy of Fine Arts	1916 Lea Prize; $100	
Boston Museum of Fine Arts, Purchase	1926 E.K. Gardner Fund	Larkspur, Peonies and Canterbury Bells
Boston Museum of Fine Arts, Purchase	1927 C.H. Hayden Fund	Yellow Dahlias
Boston Museum of Fine Arts, Purchase	1928 Lawrence Fund	The Nymph
Boston Museum of Fine Arts	15 Miniatures	Gift of the Artist

American Society of Miniature Painters	Elected Vice-President	(Founding Member)
Water Color Club		Member
Guild of Boston Artists		Member
Metropolitan Museum of Art	Purchase	Persis Blair (miniature)

Museum and Gallery Associations

American Federation of Art
American Society of Miniature Painters
Art Interchange, New York
Arden Galleries
Museum of Fine Arts, Boston
Boston Watercolor Club
Erich Galleries
Ferargil Galleries
J. Eastman Chase Gallery
Corcoran Gallery of Art
Concord Art Association
Copley Gallery
The Copley Society
Doll and Richards
Guild of Boston Artists
Knoedler's Galleries
Merrimack Valley Art Association
Metropolitan Museum of Art
National Academy of Design
Old Newbury Historical Society
Pennsylvania Academy of Fine Arts
Pennsylvania Society of Miniature Painters
Providence Art Club
Society of American Artists
Vose Galleries, Boston
Water Color Club
Woman's Art Club, New York
Woman's Industrial Union, Boston
Worcester Art Museum

The
Exhibition History
of
Laura Coombs Hills
(b. 1859 - d. 1952)

1889

J. Eastman Chase Gallery
7 Hamilton Place, Boston
Exhibition of Pastels by Laura Coombs Hills
November 14 - 23, 1889

A Late Errand
Old Fashioned Flowers
Study of a Head
He'll Come Back and Marry Me
An Irish Girl
Your Face is Your Fortune
Portrait
A Fairy Tale
The Marshes Near Newburyport
A Winter Day
Phlox
Youth
A Study of a Head (#2)
Aunt's Garden
A White Chrysanthemum
Portrait

1895

J. Eastman Chase Gallery
Seven Pretty Girls of Newburyport
Annie Brown
Alice Creasy (Crecy)
Mary Huse
Georgianna Perkins
Harriet Perkins
Ethel Reed
Elizabeth Richardson
J. Eastman Chase Gallery

Exhibition of Flower Pastels by Laura Coombs Hills
November 19 - 23, 1895

1898

Pennsylvania Academy of Fine Art
67th Annual Exhibition
Group of Miniatures

1899

Pennsylvania Academy of Fine Arts
68th Annual Exhibition
A Study in Pink
Beatrice Herford
Portrait of Sylvia
Portrait of Mrs. Charles Platt

1900

Paris Exposition
Paris, France
Laura
Dorothy
Portrait of Beatrice Herford
Portrait of Miss T.
Study in Pink

Knoedler's Galleries
First Annual Exhibition of
The American Society of Miniature Painters
January 8 - 20, 1900

Pennsylvania Academy of Fine Arts
69th Annual Exhibition
Portrait of Mrs. Ellwood Hendrick
Saint Elizabeth

Miss B.
Alice Brown

Louis Prang Company
November 23 - December 1, 1900
Roses (5)
Valentines (2)
Group of Christmas Designs

1901

Pan American Exposition
May - November, 1901

Corcoran Gallery of Art
Washington, D.C.
Fire Opal

Knoedler's Galleries, New York
American Society of Miniature Painters
February 1 - 15
(5 works, shown also in Paris)

Pennsylvania Academy of Fine Arts
70th Annual Exhibition
Study of a Head
Fire Opal

1902

Knoedler's Galleries
American Society of Miniature Painters
February 1 - 15
(6 miniatures)

1903

Knoedler's Galleries
American Society of Miniature Painters
December 27 - January 10

Pennsylvania Academy of Fine Arts
72nd Annual Exhibition
Miss May Pratt
Miss Carrie Pratt
Miss Helen Pratt
Boy Blue
Billy
Mrs. Robert Hartshorne
Mrs. George Pratt
Miss Natalie Wood
Mrs. Frederick Billings
Mrs. Thomas Motley, Jr.
Unnamed portrait

1904

Universal Exposition
St. Louis, Missouri

Water Color Club
First Exhibition, 1904
A Bowl of Zinnias
A Jar of Zinnias
Pond Lillies

Knoedler's
American Society of Miniature Painters
5th Annual Exhibition
January 1 - February 6

Water Color Club

Second Annual Exhibition, 1905
Girl in Green
Cherokee Roses
West Cedar Street

1905

Knoedler's
American Society of Miniature Painters
Fourth Annual Exhibition
Master Clement Bernheimer

1906

Water Color Club
Third Annual Exhibition

Knoedler's Galleries
Fifth Annual Exhibition
American Society of Miniature Painters
Roses
Miss 'H'
Mrs. 'B'
Miss 'C'
'M. H.'

1907

Knoedler's Galleries
Sixth Annual Exhibition of Miniatures
The Bride

1908

Copley Gallery
413 Boylston Street
Exhibition of Miniatures of Laura C. Hills
March 9 - March 21

The Red Flower

Mrs. Mayer S. Bernheimer

The Black Mantle

Miss Persis Blair

Fire Opal

Mrs. Arthur Harlow

Miss Agnes A. Childs

Miss Beatrice Herford

Mrs. John Cummings Fairchild

The Flame Girl

Saint Elizabeth

Miss Dorothy Bass Whitney

Mr. Philip Knapp Hills

Mrs. Philip Knapp Hills

Miss Lizzie Bayley Hills

Mrs. Edwin Farnham Green

Mrs. Royal Crane

Mrs. Clement Bernehimer

Miss Alice Brown

Sleeping Girl

Misses Helen and May Carey Pratt

Master Donald Moffat

Mrs. Charles A. Platt

Mrs. John Carroll Perkins

Miss Alice Josephine Morse

Miss Margaret Curzon Hale

Mrs. Robert Hartshorne

Mr. Robert Hartshorne

Miss Katherine Dreier

Master Valentine Everet Macy

Miss Elizabeth Pratt

Miss Elizabeth Pratt (#2)

Mrs. Ellwood Hendrick

Miss Mildred Howells

Miss Margorie Bernheimer

Miss Elizabeth Richardson

Miss Louise Graves

Mrs. Emmons Hamlin

Miss Dorothy Little Stevens

Miss Laura Stevens

The Bride

The Nymph

Master Philip James Roosevelt

Master William Lusk

Master John Blaney

Master Pierre Hazard

Mrs. E. C. Milliken

Dorothy

General Edward Hastings Ripley

Miss Emdeline Davis

Miss Louis Scribner

Rembrandt Gallery

Vigo Street, London

May 1908

Exhibition of Miniatures Previously Seen

at the Copley Gallery, Boston

Mary Crecy

Mrs. Mayer S. Bernheimer

Miss Dorothy Bass Whitney

Miss Marjorie B. Bernheimer

The Bride

Margaret Curzon Hale

Miss Alice Brown

1908

Worcester Art Museum

Exhibition of Miniatures by Laura Coombs Hills

November 30 - December 14, 1908

Miss Dorothy Bass Whitney

Miss Alice Brown

Mr. Philip Knapp Hills

Miss Elizabeth Richardson

Miss Lizzie Bayley Hills

Dorothy

Mrs. Philip Knapp Hills

Miss Laura Stevens

Sleeping Girl

Mr. Clement Bernheimer

Miss Agnes A. Childs

Saint Elizabeth

Mrs. John Cummings Fairchild

Miss Elizabeth Pratt

Miss Marjorie Bernheimer

Miss Mary Louise Miller

Miss Alice Josephine Morse

Miss Dorothy Little Stevens

Mrs. H. Dewey

The Flame Girl

Fire Opal

Miss Louise Graves

Mr. Arthur Harlow

Mrs. Royal Crane

Miss Persis Blair

The Black Mantle

The Bride

Miss Bertrice Herford

The Nymph

Mrs. Mayer B. Bernheimer

The Red Flower

Miss Margaret Curzon Hale

1909

Water Color Club
Seventh Annual Exhibition

Knoedler's Gallery
Eight Annual Miniature Exhibition

Portrait of Miss G.

The Nymph

Margaret Curzon Hale

Unnamed portrait

1910

Copley Gallery

Miniatures by Laura Coombs Hills

January 15 - February 7

Psyche

Portrait of Miss Bertha Coolidge

Girl with Violets

A Study

A Portrait

Master George Glover Crocker

Master Thomas Liffingwell Shipman

Miss Margaret Curzon Hale

The Yellow Scarf

Portrait

The Bride

Fire Opal

Little Agnes

Study of A Blonde

A Study

A Blonde Profile

Portrait

Master Grosvenor Ely, Jr.

Blue Bandeau

Portrait

Portrait

The Nymph

Persis Blair

The Black Mantle

The Red Flower

Portrait

1910

Water Color Club
Eighth Annual Exhibit

Knoedler's Galleries
Ninth Annual Miniature Exhibition
Flowers in the Sunshine
Portrait of Master John Edsall
The Yellow Scarf

1911

Water Color Club
Ninth Annual Exhibition
The Tea Table
White Petunias

1912

Water Color Club
Tenth Annual Exhibition
Portraits (2)

Pennsylvania Academy of Fine Arts
Miniatures (8)

1913

Water Color Club
Eleventh Annual Exhibition

1914

Guild of Boston Artists
First General Exhibit
November 2 - November 14
Miniatures (4)

Water Color Club
Twelveth Annual Show

Pennsylvania Academy of Fine Arts
13th Annual Exhibition of Miniatures

American Society of Miniature Painters
15th Annual Exhibition,
at the National Academy of Design
March 21 - April 26, 1914

Royal Society of Miniature Painters
London, England
May - June

1915

Panama Pacific International Exposition
Little Agnes
Girl with Violets
Margaret Curzon Hale
The Nymph
Psyche
The Morning Cup
Portrait

Guild of Boston Artists
Second General Exhibition

Guild of Boston Artists
May 3 - 15

Guild of Boston Artists
Traveling Show

Guild of Boston Artists
Fourteenth Annual Miniature Exhibition

November 5 - December 10
White and Gold
Portrait of Edward Everett Hale, 3rd
Catherine Arms Everett

Pennsylvania Academy of Fine Art
Fifteenth Annual Miniature Exhibit

1916

Inactive

1917

Pennsylvania Academy of Fine Art
16th Exhibit of Miniatures
November and December
Miss Jane L. Everett
Miss Katherine Everett

1918

Pennsylvania Academy of Fine Arts
17th Annual Miniature Exhibit
The Black Hat

1919

Pennsylvania Academy of Fine Art
18th Annual Miniature Exhibit
Elizabeth Rutter

American Society of Miniature Painters
Buffalo Academy of Fine Arts
December - January 5
Miniatures (6)

1920

Pennsylvania Academy of Fine Arts
Eighteenth Annual Exhibition
Water Color Club

Pennsylvania Academy of Fine Arts
19th Annual Miniature Exhibit
November 7 - December 12

Guild of Boston Artists
Sixth Annual Exhibit
May

1921

Guild of Boston Artists
Seventh Annual Exhibit
May

Pennsylvania Academy of Fine Art
Philadelphia Water Color Club

1922

Concord Art Association
Fire and Ashes

Paris Exposition
The Bride
Little Agnes
Margaret Curzon Hale
Mary Crecy
Edward Everett Hale, 3rd
Fire Opal

Guild of Boston Artists
Private Viewing
January 23rd.

1923

Guild of Boston Artists
Ninth Annual Show

Guild of Boston Artists
Exhibit of Miniatures

1924

Pennsylvania Academy of Fine Art
23rd Annual Exhibition
Mary Swan
Mrs. Basil de Selincourt
(Anne Sedgewick Douglas)
Elizabeth Swan

1925

American Society of Miniature Painters
26th Annual Exhibition
at Erich Galleries
January 27 - February 11, 1925
Marjorie Prince
Elizabeth Swan
Mary Swan

Guild of Boston Artists
Exhibition of Miniatures of Laura C. Hills
February 2 - March 7, 1925
Henry Vaughn
Crimson and Blue
Mrs. William Ellery

Miss Frances Biddie
Anne Douglas Sedgewick

1926

American Society of Miniature Painters
27th Annual Exhibition
Hills declined.

Copley Gallery
Exhibition of Pastels of Flowers
November 22 - December 11
(Forty-four works submitted)

1927

American Society of Miniature Painters
Twenty-sixth Annual Exhibition
Mme. Berenstrieff

American Society of Miniature Painters
Twenty-eighth Annual Exhibition
at MacBeth Galleries
Helen Harlow

1928

Copley Gallery
103 Newbury Street
Exhibition of Pastels of Flowers by Laura Coombs Hills
At Anne Hathaways
White Freesia
Pink Roses
A Little Jazz
English Daisies and Forget-Me-Nots
Apple Blossoms
Pansies
Little Bowl of Flowers

Apple Blossoms and Silver

White Roses

Calendulas

Daffodils

Columbine

Hillside Iris

White Peonies

Pink and Lavendar

Roses and Larkspur

Tulips

Peonies and Pyrethrums

Zinnias

Sunnyside Gladiolas

Larkspur and Lilies

Dahlias and Campanulas

Large Bowl of Flowers

Roses

Convolvulus Minor

The Wreath

White Petunias and Silver

Basket of Flowers

Poppies and Honey Pots

Marsh Marigolds

Lilium Azuratum

White Petunias

Little Bowl of Flowers

Tea Roses

Zinnias and Green

Dahlias and Copper

Nicotinas at Night

Dark Petunias

Bowl of Dahlias

1929

Inactive

1930

Pennsylvania Academy of Fine Arts
Twenty-ninth Annual Miniature Exhibit
Mrs. Roger Warren

1931

Copley Gallery
Exhibition of Pastels of Flowers
November 16 - December 15
30 works exhibited

1932

Doll and Richards
Exhibit of Pastels of Flowers by Laura Coombs Hills
November 14 - December 2
Peonies
Yellow Roses
Marigolds
White Roses
White Peonies and Rocket
Flowers in A Yellow jar
Mixed Flowers with Blue Background
Zinnias and Brass
Mixed Flowers in White Jar
Pansies and Rose
Flowers and Gray Velvet
Small Bowl of Zinnias
Larkspur and Cosmos
Apple Blossoms
Primroses
Pansies
White Phlox in Sunshine
Gilliflowers and Petunias
Crimson Rose

1933

Doll and Richards
Exhibition of Flower Pastels
November 6 - 25
(23 works sold)

Pennsylvania Society of Miniature Painters
23rd Annual Exhibition
Eleanor Pickering Randall

Boston Art Club
January 9 - 28
Tulips

Doll and Richards
Exhibit of Pastels of Flowers by Laura Coombs Hills
November 14 - December 2

1934

Doll and Richards
Exhibit of Pastels of Flowers by Laura Coombs Hills
November 13 - December 1
The May Queen
Zinnias
Petunias
Petunias, No. 2
Chiniensis and Lilies
Stocks and Petunias
The Little Bouquet
Night Blooming Cereus
White Petunias
Larkspur and Lilies
White Roses
Yellow Roses
Apple Blossoms

Salpiglossis

Pansies

Early Spring

Red Lilies

Iris

June Flowers

Peonies

Basket of Fruit

Cherokee Roses

Calla Lilies

The Rapture Rose

Flowers in White Jar

Little Bowl of Roses

Yellow Rose

Red and White Camellia

White Music

Daffodils

The Little Green One

1935

Doll and Richards

Exhibition of Pastels of Flowers by Laura Coombs Hills

November 9 - November 30

White Roses

Flowering Crab Apple

Yellow Roses

Larkspur and Lilies

In the Woods

Peonies

Pansies

White Jar of Yellow Roses

Pink Ross

Yellow Nasturtiums

White Phlox in the Sunshine

Petunias and Gypsophilia

Bowl of Mixed Flowers

Three Roses
Yellow Pansies
Zinnias and Stock
Marigolds and Pewter
Snowberries Against Green
Fall Flowers
The Spanish Bowl
Roses and Larkspur
Pond Liles
Night Blooming Cereus
Pond Lily
Yellow Freesia
Flower in White Jar
Shirley Poppies
Tulips

1936

Doll and Richards
November 9 - 28, 1936
(28-32 works sold)

Vose Galleries, Boston
(Two pastels sold)

1937

Doll and Richards
Exhibition of Pastels of Flowers by Laura Coombs Hills
November 8 - 27, 1937

1938

Doll and Richards
Exhibition of Pastels of Flowers
November 8 - 27, 19378
(19 works sold)

1939

Doll and Richards
Exhibition of Pastels of Flowers
November 13 - December 2, 1939

1940

Doll and Richards
Exhibition of Pastels of Flowers By Laura Coombs Hills
November 12 - 27, 1940

Ferargil Gallerie, New York
March 11 - 24, 1940
30 Pastels

1941

Guild of Boston Artists
Exhibition of Pastels of Flowers
November 24 - December 6
Van Fleet Roses
Iris
Flowery Firmament
Begonias
Breakfast
White Petunias
Pansies
Zinnias and Stock
Tulips
Daffodils
Summer Amaryllis
Tulips
Queen Mary Rose and English Ivy
Zinnias and Copper
Begonias
The Vine

Snow Berries
Red and White Roses
Basket of Fruit
Drummond Phlox
Peonies and Glass
Morning
Bowl of Flowers
White Jar of Flowers
White Roses
Peonies
June Flowers
Harrison Roses

Guild of Boston Artists
Larkspur and Lilies
Petunias
Zinnias

1942

Guild of Boston Artists
Exhibition of Pastels of Flowers
November 23 - December 5
Yellow Roses
Two Yellow Roses
Little Roses
Primrose
Mixed Flowers
Tulips by Lamp Light
White Roses
Harrison Roses
Van Fleet Roses
Pink and Yellow
Summer Flowers
A Van Fleet Rose
Zinnias and Stock
Pond Lilies

Yellow Pansies

Roses and Pinks

Yellow Freezias

Lilies and Iris

Mixed Flowers

Tulips and Freezias

Apple Blossoms

Pansies

Peonies

Pale Pansies

Lilliputs

Sun Flowers

Blue and White

Mid-Day

The Hurricane

1943

Guild of Boston Artists

Exhibition of Pastels of Flowers

November 29 - December 18

(28 works sold)

Little Yellow Roses

Florist's Flowers

Yellow Roses

Spring Flowers

The Pink Camellia

White and Blue

Flowering Crab

White Roses

Harrison Roses

Little Green Bowl

Peonies and Glass

White Against White

Mixed Flowers

Larkspur and Lilies

Poppies, Calendulas and Euphobia

Larkspur and White Iris

Bowl of Zinnias

White Petunias

Pottery from Peru

The May Queen

Macaw

Garland of Roses

White Jar of Flowers

Spilled Poppies

Petunias and Pewter

Ladies Delight

Heavenly Blues

Drummond Phlox

1944

Guild of Boston Artists

Exhibition of Pastels of Flowers

November 27 - December 9, 1944

1945

Guild of Boston Artists

Retrospective Exhibition of Pastels of Flowers

by Laura Coombs Hills

November 26 - December 15, 1945

Rhododendrons

Zinnias and Stock

Morning

Gladiolas

Breakfast

Roses and Pinks

Yellow Roses

Tulips and Freezia

Spilled Poppies

Pink and Yellow

Pink Dahlias

Larkspur and Lilies

Evening

Larkspur and White Iris

Lilliputs

Marigolds in the Sunshine

Tulips

Peonies

Iris

Yellow Freezia

Basket of Fruit

Mid-Day

Dark Petunias

Pond Lilies

Zinnias and Copper

Queen Mary Roses and English Ivy

Petunias and Pewter

Florist's Flowers

White Petunias

1946

Guild of Boston Artists

Exhibition of Pastels of Flowers

November 17 - December 6, 1946

(Partial list of works available)

(31 works sold)

White Ross

English Primrose

Van Fleets

Shirley Poppies

Pink Dahlias

Larkspur and Lilies

1949

H. W. Prays Department Store
Newburyport, Massachusetts
Exhibition of Antique Doll of Laura Coombs Hills
'Patricia'

2001

Guild of Boston Artists
A Woman's Perspective: Founding and Early
Women Members of the Guild of Boston Artists, 1914-1945
(A retrospective show)

2009

Lepore Fine Arts Newburyport &
The Cooley Gallery, Connecticut,
Portraits from My Garden
November 12, 2009 at the
Boston International Fine Art Show;
November 21 - January 2, 2010 at the
Cooley Gallery.

Index to Reproductions

The Black Hat

Williamson, G.C. and Buckman, P., Royal Miniature Society. The Art of the Miniature Painter. "Miss Laura Combs Hills of Boston, U.S.A.", Chapman and Hall, Ltd. (London: 1926) p. 238.

Persis Blair

Boston Museum of Fine Arts, untitled article, vertical files.
Clement, Clara. Women in the Fine Arts;
Isham, Samuel. History of American Painting. The MacMillan Company. 1927.

Mrs. Edwin Blashfield

Nuttell, Grace Alexander, "A Painter of Miniatures", The Puritan, Vol. V., April 1899, No. 3, p. 1 in American Artists, Vol. 111, A-Z, 989. (Twelve works reproduced here: including: Sister and Brother; Mrs. Charles Platt; Mrs. Sidney Haywood (Miss Beatrice Herford); Miss Grace Hall; Miss Georgiana Perkins; Mrs. Edwin H. Blashfield; A Study in Pink; Dorothy; Miss Francis Morris; Self-Portrait of Miss Laura Coombs Hills; Portrait of Mrs. T.; Laura; p. 988, 366; 387; 388; 389;)

The Butterfly Girl

Duncan, Frances. "The Miniatures of Miss Laura Combs Hills", International Studio, Vol. 41, August 1910, p. xlvi-xlviii. Vol. 41, 1910.

Runge, Clara. "The Tonal School of America", International Studio, Vol. 27, January 1906, LXVII-LXVI; ref. in Gerdts, William. *American Impressionism.*

Mrs. George W. Chadwick

     American Magazine of Art, 1928, p. 459.

Daffodils (miniature)

     American Magazine of Art, 1928.

Dorothy

     Nuttell, Grace Alexander, op.cit.

Miss Jane Everett

     American Magazine of Art, 1928.

The Fire Opal

     International Studio, p. xlvii.

Girl with Violets

     American Magazine of Art, p. 459.

The Goldfish (Newburyport Girl with Flowing Red Tresses)

     Boston Museum of Art, periodical, unknown source.

Miss Ruth Graves

     American Magazine of Art.

Miss Margaret Curzon Hale

     American Magazine of Art, p. 460.

Miss Grace Hall

     Nuttell, Grace Alexander. "A Painter of Miniatures", The Puritan, Vol. V, April 1899, No. 3, p. 1 in American Artists, Vol. 111, A-Z 989.

Portrait of Arthur Harlow

Duncan, Francis. "The Miniatures of Miss Laura Coombs Hills", op.cit.

Mrs. Sidney Haywood (Miss Beatrice Herford)

Nuttell, Grace Alexander. "A Painter of Miniatures", op.cit.

Larkspur, Peonies, and Canterbury Bells

American Magazine of Art, 1928.

Little Agnes

American Magazine of Art, p. 458.

Laura

Nuttell, Grace Alexander, "A Painter of Miniatures", op.cit.

Miss Francis Morris

Nuttell, Grace Alexander, "A Painter of Miniatures", op.cit.

Pansies

Doll and Richards, Catalogue, Cover, December 9, 1936.

Pastel of Flowers

Arts and Artists. Unknown date.

Miss Georgianna Perkins

Nuttell, Grace Alexander, "A Painter of Miniatures", op.cit.

Dark Petunias

Guild of Boston Artists, Catalogue, Cover, November 18, 1946.

Mrs. Charles Platt

> Nuttell, Grace Alexander, "A Painter of Miniatures", op.cit.

Pond Lilies

> Guild of Boston Artists, Catalogue, Cover, November 18,1945.

Portrait (of a young lady in dress)

> Duncan, Frances. "The Miniatures of Miss Laura Hills", op.cit.

Roses

> Copley Gallery, Exhibition Catalogue, Cover, November 1926.

Roses

> Guild of Boston Artists, Catalogue, Cover, November 24, 1941.

Roses

> Guild of Boston Artists, Catalogue, Cover, December 5, 1942.

Roses

> Guild of Boston Artists, Catalogue, Cover, November 29, 1943.

Elizabeth Rutter

> American Magazine of Art, 1928.

Self-Portrait of Miss Laura Coombs Hills

> Nuttell, Grace Alexander, "A Painter of Miniatures", op. cit.

Sister and Brother

> Nuttell, Grace Alexander, "A Painter of Miniatures", op.cit.

A Study in Pink

        Nuttell, Grace Alexander, "A Painter of Miniatures", op.cit.

Portrait of Mrs. T.

        Nuttell, Grace Alexander, "A Painter of Miniatures", op.cit.

Miss Dorothy Whitney of Newburyport

        Boston Museum of Fine Arts, periodical, unknown source.
        Yellow Pansies
        Ferargil Gallery, Catalogue, "Laura Coombs Hills", 1940.

The Yellow Scarf

        American Magazine of Art, p. 459.

Endnotes

Introduction

1 Definition taken from The Free Dictionary.com/lyricism.
2 Definition taken from The Free Dictionary.com/lyricism.
3 Definition taken from: https://www.dictionary.com/brouse/lyrical
4 Dictionary.Cambridge.org/us/dictionary/English/lyricism.
5 Https://www.vocabulary.com/dictionary/lyrical.
6 Https://www.1doceonline.com/music.topic//Lyricism.
7 Eleanor Roberts. "Flower Artist at 91 Finds Work Still in Demand - - Has Won Many Medals", Boston Sunday Post. April 8, 1951.

Biography - Life in Newburyport

8 Diane Kelleher. KRN:LCH. Especially, Bureau of Vital Statistics, Certificate of Death of Laura Coombs Hills, 1952. Other information in this paragraph is from: The Historical Society of Old Newbury: Essex County Courthouse Records including Will #236902, February 27, 1952.
9 Eleanor Roberts. "Flower Artist at 91 Finds Work Still in Demand - - Has Won Many Medals", Boston Sunday Post, April 8, 1951.
10 Robert C. Vose, Jr. Speech to the Old Newbury Historical Society, "The Dual Lives of Laura Coombs Hills, at the Centenary Anniversary. Text draws upon Eleanor Roberts article appearing in the Boston Sunday Post, April, 1951.
11 Eleanor Roberts. Ibid. April 8, 1951.
12 KRN:LCH, Historical Society of Old Newbury, records on Laura Coombs Hills, p. 9.
13 Freida Marion. "Artist Exhibits Antique Doll", unknown paper; Laura Coombs Hills. Letter to Mildred Howells dated September 26, 1951.
14 Grace Nuttell. "A Painter of Miniatures", The Puritan, Vol. V. No. 3, April 1899, in *American Artists, ed., Vol. III, A-Z*. Also "Time and the Hour".
15 _____. Ibid.
16 Unknown author. Time and the Hour, May 22, 1897.
17 Diane Kelleher. KRN:LCH, p. 4.
18 _____. Ibid. Re: *Chromolithographs of Louis Prang*, p. 4.
19 _____. Ibid. Re: Trip to Europe with Oliver, p. 5; also Vose, Robert. "Laura Coombs Hills" Centenary Speech to Old Newbury Historical Society.
20 Unknown author. "Laura Coombs Hills", American Magazine of Art, undated, in KRN:LCH.

21 Railroad industry histories obtainable at Boston Public Library, Boston, Massachusetts.

22 Eleanor Roberts. Op. cit.

23 _____. Ibid.

24 Biographical Sketches of American Artists, Michigan State Library, 1924; Kelleher, KRN:LCH, p. 37, 101, 105; Vose. Op.cit.

25 Laura Fairchild Fuller. "Modern American Miniature Painters", Scribner's Magazine, 1920.

26 Eleanor Roberts. Op.cit; Kelleher. Op.cit., p. 21.

27 Dorothea Mann. "Laura Coombs Hills", Art and Artists, December 1936, states 22 commissions emerged from "Seven Pretty Girls of Newburyport" rather than 27 as elsewhere stated., c.f. Kelleher, KRN:LCH, p. 130; J. Eastman Chase Gallery Exhibition.

28 Mantle Fielding. *Dictionary of American Painters, Sculptors, and Engravers,* 1926.

29 Bernadine Kielty, ed. *A Treasury of Short Stories.* "The Hilton's Holiday", Sarah Orne Jewett. Simon and Schuster (New York: 1947) p. 263-275.

30 Roberts. Op.cit.

31 _____. Ibid.

32 Unknown author. Craftsman Magazine. "The House That Has the Quality of an Old Homestead: Built by Laura Coombs Hills at Newburyport", unknown date.

33 Roberts. Op.cit.

34 *Who's Who in American Art, Vol. 1, 1936-37.*

35 Unknown author. Craftsman Magazine. Op.cit.

36 _____. Ibid.

37 Robert Vose. "Laura Coombs Hills" speech to Newburyport Historical Society, American Magazine of Art, in KRN:LCH.

38 Robert Vose. "Laura Coombs Hills" speech to Newburyport Historical Society, American Magazine of Art, in KRN:LCH.

39 Robert Vose. "Laura Coombs Hills" speech to Newburyport Historical Society, American Magazine of Art, in KRN:LCH.

40 Robert Vose. "Laura Coombs Hills" speech to Newburyport Historical Society, American Magazine of Art, in KRN:LCH.

41 Robert Vose. "Laura Coombs Hills" speech to Newburyport Historical Society, American Magazine of Art, in KRN:LCH.

42 Fielding, Op.cit.: *Who's Who in American Art, Vol. 1, 1936-37.*

43 Fielding, Op.cit.: *Who's Who in American Art, Vol. 1, 1936-37.*

44 Fielding, Op.cit.: *Who's Who in American Art, Vol. 1, 1936-37.*

45 Roberts. Op.cit.

46 Roberts. Op.cit.

47 Roberts. Op.cit.

48 Roberts. Op.cit.

49 Copley Gallery. Exhibition catalogue, November 12 - December 4, 1926.

50 Roberts. Op.cit.

51 Laura Coombs Hills. Letter to Mildred Howells dated June 13, 1950.

52 Roberts. Op.cit.

53 _____. Ibid.

54 Freida Marion. "Artists Exhibits Antique Doll". Old Newbury Historical Society.

55 Vose. Op.cit.

56 Hills. Letter to Mildred Howells dated August 1930.

57 Roberts. Op.cit.; Laura Hills' book, "Genealogical Data, Ancestry, and Descendants of William Hills, 1632.

58 Freida Marion. "Artist Exhibits Antique Doll".

59 Unknown author. Craftsman Magazine. Op.cit.

60 Roberts. Op.cit.

61 _____. Ibid.

62 Hills. Letter to Mildred Howells dated June 13, 1950.

63 _____. Ibid.

64 _____. Ibid.

65 Eleanor Roberts. Op.cit.

66 William Gerdts. *American Impressionism*. Henry Art Gallery. 1980.

67 Henry Nash Smith. *Virgin Land: The American West as Symbol and Myth*. Harvard University Press. Cambridge, Massachusetts. 1970.

68 Aristotle. *Politics*.

69 Page Smith. *Daughters of the Promised Land*. Little, Brown. Boston. 1970.

70 Ovid. *The Art of Love*.

71 Page Smith. Op.cit.

72 Louisa May Alcott. *Little Women*.

73 Henry James. *The Portrait of a Lady*.

74 Mark Twain. *Innocents Abroad.*.

75 Gerdts. Op.cit.

76 Page Smith. Op.cit.

77 _____. Ibid.

78 _____. Ibid.

79 Guild of Boston Artists. Archives of American Art. Boston Herald newspaper, art editorial. March 7, 1915.

80 Kelleher. *Enchantment: The Art and Life of Lilian Westcott Hale*.

81 Boston Traveller. "Laura Coombs Hills". February 21, 1952.

82 United Press. "Laura C. Hills, Noted Artist, Dead at 93", February 21, 1952.

Abbreviations:

KRN:LCH = Kelleher Research Notes on Laura Coombs Hills

KRN:LWH = Kelleher Research Notes on Lilian Westcott Hale.

Marvelous Miniatures

83 Walt Whitman. *The Selected Poems of Walt Whitman*. Walter J. Black (New York: 1942).

84 Charles Elliot. *English Poetry, Harvard Classics Series, Vol. 41*. P.F. Collier and Son, Corp. (New York: 1938, 1956).

85 Isabel Quigly. *Shelley*. Penguin Books. (Baltimore: 1956).

86 Elliot. Op.cit., Vol. 41, p. 789.

87 _____. Ibid., p. 821.

88 _____. Ibid., p. 534

89 _____. Ibid., p. 534.

90 _____. Ibid., p. 474.

91 _____. Ibid., p. 1040.

92 Edmund Burke. "A Philosophical Inquiry into Origins of Our Ideas of the Sublime and the Beautiful"; On Taste" p. 1-140 in Charles Elliot, LL.D., ed. *The Harvard Classics, Vol. 24.* P.F. Collier and Son, Corp. (New York: 1909; pps. 75, 77, 92, 97, 105.

93 _____. Ibid., p. 92.

94 _____. Ibid., p. 97.

95 Encyclopedia Britannica, Vol. 8. William Benton, Publishers. (Chicago: 1963). P. 572-594; esp. 591-594.

96 Baruch Spinoza. "The Good Emotions", in KRN:LCH.

97 Unknown newspaper. KRN:LCH, 1977/8.

98 William Dunlap. "History of Miniature Painting", *History of the Arts of Design in the United States,* p. 14, 244, 414.

99 _____., p. 296-298.

100 _____., p. 224.

101 AE. Unknown paper. [Queen of Miniature Painters], KRN:LCH.

102 William Dunlap. Op.cit., T.S. Cummings "Practical Directions for Miniature Painting", p. 10-14.

103 _____., *History, Vol. II, Part 2,* pl. 380. [Sally Solomon]

104 _____. Ibid., pl. 291, p. 380. [Mrs. Hurtell]

105 _____. Ibid., pl. 281, p. 370. [Hall group]

106 _____. Ibid., p. 309, p. 402. [Cook]

107 AE. Unknown author, untitled, Boston Herald, May 9, 1915 [John Singer Sargent of Miniature Painting]

108 Diane Kelleher. KRN:LCH. [mechanic arts]

109 _____. *Enchantment: The Art and Life of Lilian Westcott Hale,* Author House, 2013.

110 _____. KRN:LCH.

111 _____., Ibid., [Re: Carolus Duran]

112 _____., Ibid. [water color and pastels as finished mediums].

113 Sandra B. Lepore. "Breaking the Accepted rules of Color" in Exhibition Catalogue *Laura Coombs Hills: Portraits From My Garden.* Cooley Gallery, Old Lyme, Connecticut.

114 Maryanne Sudnick Gunderson. *Dismissed Yet Disarming: The Portrait Miniature Revival, 1890-1930.* Ohio University. (Ohio: 2003). P. 15.

115 _____. Ibid. p. 19.

116 _____. Ibid. p. 21.

117 _____. Ibid. p. 9.

118 _____. Ibid. p. 91-92.

119 _____. Ibid. p. 31.

120 _____. Ibid. p. 31.

121 _____. Ibid. p. 49-51.

122 Leila Mechlin. "Laura Coombs Hills", American Magazine of Art, unknown date.

123 Grace Nuttell. "A Painter of Miniatures.", 1899, Vol. V., No. 3.

124 Unknown author. *American Artists, Biographical Sketches*. Michigan State Library, p. 192.

125 AE. Unknown source.

126 AE. Journal. May 4, 1915.

127 AE. Providence Journal, May 16, 1916.

128 AE. Boston Advertiser, May 6, 1915.

129 AE. Boston Herald, May 9, 1915.

130 AE. Boston Herald, March 7, 1915.

131 AE. Transcript, May 1915.

132 AE. Boston Herald, May 2, 1915.

133 AE. Boston Globe, May 5, 1915.

134 Unknown paper, 1921. KRN:LCH.

135 Lucia Fairchild Fuller. "Modern American Miniature Painters", Scribner's Magazine, 1920.

136 Florence Spaulding. "Laura Coombs Hills". Arts and Artists, ed. Dorothea Mann, December 1936.

137 Frances Duncan. "Miniatures By Miss Hills", International Studio, p. XLVI, XLVIII.

138 AE. Untitled. International Studio, 1910.

139 Grace Alexander Nuttell. "A Painter of Miniatures", The Puritan, Vol. V, April 1899 in American Artists, Vol. III A-Z, No. 3, p. 1.

140 _____. Ibid. p. 1.

141 Duncan, Op.cit., "Miniatures by Miss Hills", p. XLVIII.

142 _____. "Laura Coombs Hills", American Magazine of Art.

143 AE. Boston Herald, May 9, 1915.

144 AE. Boston Herald, May 9, 1915; and *Biographical Sketches of American Artists*.

145 Unknown author. *Biographical Sketches of American Artists, 1924:* AE. Boston Transcript, unknown date.

146 _____. Ibid.

147 _____. Ibid.

148 Clara Clement. *Women in the Fine Arts*, 1895.

149 AE. Boston Herald, May 9, 1915.

*Note: Abbreviations:

AE=Art Editorial; KRN:LCH=Kelleher Research Notes on L.C. Hills

Many tidbits of information arrived with only partial source notations, so some individual entries may be incomplete.

Perfect Pastels

150 Internet. Invaluable.com/artist/hills-laura-coombs-owp8xa900h/sold at auction prices. Retrieved July 12, 2020.

151 _____. Ibid.

152 Internet. Widewalls.ch/magazine/1920s art. Retrieved July 12, 2020.

153 Internet. Artic.edu/exhibitions/1952/America-after-the-fall-painting in the 1930s. Retrieved July 12, 2020.

154 _____. Ibid.

155 _____. Ibid.

156 _____. Ibid.

157 Theodore E. Stebbins, Jr. *American Master Drawings and Watercolors*. Harper and Rowe Publishers (New York: 1976) p. 26. [re: Henrietta Johnston,]

158 _____. Ibid. p. 10, 26.

159 _____. Ibid., p. 10, 26-28.

160 _____. Ibid.

161 _____. Ibid.

162 AE. Herald, May 9, 1915.

163 Gerdts. "John Singer Sargent and the Beginning of Impressionist Painting in America", *American Impressionism*, p. 37-45 [re: William Morris Hunt].

164 _____. Ibid., p. 18.

165 _____. Ibid., pps. 17-19, 24, 40, 58.

166 AE. Untitled article. KRN:LCH.

167 Faber Birren. *Principles of Color: A Review of Past Traditions and Modern Theories of Color Harmony*. Schiffer Publishing. (Atglen, Pennsylvania: 1987). P. 10.

168 _____. Ibid., p. 77.

169 Walt Whitman. *The Selected Poems of Walt Whitman*. Walker J. Black (New York: 1942).

170 Faber Birren. Op. cit., pps. 9-20.

171 Faber Birren. Op. cit., pps. 9-20.

172 Faber Birren. Op. cit., pps. 9-20.

173 Faber Birren. Op. cit., pps. 9-20.

174 Faber Birren. Op. cit., pps. 9-20.

175 Faber Birren. Op. cit., pps. 9-20.

176 Faber Birren. Op. cit., pps. 9-20.

177 Faber Birren. Op. cit., pps. 9-20.

178 Birren. *Color Theory for Designers, Part I: The Meaning of Color*. KRN:LCH.

179 Stebbins, Op.cit. p. 23.

180 Sandra B. Lepore. "Breaking the Accepted Rules of Color" in Exhibition Catalogue titled *Laura Coombs Hills: Portraits From My Garden*.

181 Internet. ARTSY. "The 19th C. French Academy". Retrieved 7/14/20.

182 Edmund Burke. *A Philosophical Inquiry Into the Origins of Our Ideas of the Sublime and the Beautiful* in *The Harvard Classics*. Vol. 24. ed. By Charles Eliot, LL.D., P.F. Collier and Sons, Corp. (New York: 1909).

183 Birren. Ibid., p. 8.

184 Lepore. Op.cit.

185 Birren. Ibid., p. 17. [Brewsterian color wheel]

186 _____. Ibid., p. 18 and 19. [Printer's color wheel -CMY]

187 Kelleher. KRN:LCH. The Transformation of Landscape Painting in France.

188 Michel Eugene Chevreul. *The Principles of Harmony and Contrast of Colors and Their Application to the Arts.* P. 141-146.

189 Michel Eugene Chevreul. *The Principles of Harmony and Contrast of Colors and Their Application to the Arts.* P. 141-146.

190 Michel Eugene Chevreul. *The Principles of Harmony and Contrast of Colors and Their Application to the Arts.* P. 141-146.

191 Michel Eugene Chevreul. *The Principles of Harmony and Contrast of Colors and Their Application to the Arts.* P. 141-146.

192 Michel Eugene Chevreul. *The Principles of Harmony and Contrast of Colors and Their Application to the Arts.* P. 141-146.

193 Michel Eugene Chevreul. *The Principles of Harmony and Contrast of Colors and Their Application to the Arts.* P. 141-146.

194 Birren. Op.cit. p. 30-37.

195 Birren. Op.cit. p. 30-37.

196 Birren. Op.cit. p. 30-37.

197 Birren. Op.cit. p. 30-37.

198 Birren. Op.cit. p. 30-37.

199 _____. Ibid., p. 38.

200 Chevreul. Op.cit. p. 51.

201 Internet. Bruce MacEvoy "Michel-Eugene Chevreul's Principles of Color Harmony and Contrast." KRN:LCH.

202 Birren. Op.cit. p. 40-43.

203 Birren. Op.cit. p. 40-43.

204 Birren. Op.cit. p. 40-43.

205 Birren. Op.cit. p. 40-43.

206 Birren. Op.cit. p. 40-43.

207 _____. Ibid., p. 53.

208 _____. Ibid., p. 66.

Perfect Pastels: The Critics

209 United Press, 1940, "Laura Coombs Hills".

210 Sunday Post, undated article, "Zinnias and Copper".

211 United Press Review, undated, untitled article: "...past 8, without peer."

212 United Press Review, March 29, 1943, re: Annual Guild of Boston Arts Exhibition.

213 Boston Herald, December 1944, re: exhibition, Hills, age 84.

214 Boston Herald, December 5, 1943 (Guild of Boston Artists).

215 United Press, untitled, 1940.

216 American Art Annual, 1925. "Laura Coombs Hills Show".

217 AE. A.J. Philpott, "Flower Painting Exhibition Attracts Enthusiasts".

218 AE. Untitled, undated article.

Bibliography

Abbreviations:
AE = Art Editorial;
KRN:LCH = Kelleher Research Notes for Laura Coombs Hills
BMFA = Museum of Fine Arts, Boston
UP = Unknown Paper; UD = Unknown Date; UA = Untitled Article

AE. "Laura Coombs Hills", UP dated 1940, located at Old Newbury Historical Society Newburyport MA.

AE. "Laura Hills Centenary Will Be Marked By Special Exhibit", UP, 1959.

AE. "Benjamin Pierce Lathrop House Back in Family With Latest Sale", Progress Today Newspaper, September 11, 1959.

AE. The Record, UA, November 18, 1914.

AE. Sunday Post, UA, October 27 - November 29, 1942.

AE. Review of Sunday Post article, UP, 1942.

AE. Review of Guild of Boston Artists' Annual Exhibit, UP, dated March 29, 1943.

AE. Boston Herald, UA, December 5, 1943.

AE. "Another Little House Planned By A Woman: The Home of Miss Laura C. Hills, the Painter of Miniatures, Newburyport, Mass.", unknown author, UP, UD, p. 99.

AE. "Laura Coombs Hills' Show", Christian Science Monitor, November 25, 1947.

AE. Boston Sunday Herald, UA, January 24, 1904.

AE.   Boston Herald, UA, November 23, 1939.

AE.   New England Home Magazine, UA, March 12, 1898.

AE.   Boston Herald, UA, May 9, 1915.

AE.   Boston Transcript, UA, May 1915.

AE.   Journal, UA, May 1915.

AE.   Providence Journal, UA, May 16, 1915.

AE.   "Garden Club Member", UP, 1959.

AE.   "Laura Coombs Hills Exhibit Centenary Will Be Marked By Special Exhibit at which R. Vose Will Speak", July 16, 1959, from files at Newbury Historical Society.

AE.   New England Home Magazine, April 1899.

AE.   "The Pageant of the Year at Boston's Mechanics Hall", The Puritan, April 18, 1899.

AE.   "Pennsylvania Society of Miniature Painters", International Studio, 1922-23, Vol. 41, Sup., XIV.

AE.   "Dual Talent of Laura Hills Cited by Vose Gallery Man", Newburyport, Massachusetts Daily News, July 16, 1959.

AE.   "Early American Engraved Portraits", UP, UD.

AE.   "Laura Coombs Hills, including reproduction of Yellow Pansies, at Old Newbury Historical Society, Massachusetts", UP, UD.

AE.   Boston Herald, UA, May 2, 1915.

AE.   Boston Globe, UA, May 5, 1915.

AE.   New York Herald, UA, 1940.

American Art Journal. Entry for "Hills, Laura": 1898, 1903, 1904, 1915, 1925, 1927.

American Art News. Vol. 4, December 1905, p. 2.

Art Amateur, No. 2 & 3, July and August 1882, 1877.

American Artists. Vol. V: Z-A, April 1899, 1924, No. 3.

American Magazine of Art, February 26, 1928, p. 108.

_____. "Laura Coombs Hills, Miniature Painting", 1891, p. 401-461.
_____. "Laura Coombs Hills", p. 458-461.

Art Annual, 1900-1901. Vol. III

Art Institute of Chicago. *Art Institute of Chicago Index to Periodicals. Vol. 5. Giam-Indians, I; Scrapbooks, Vol. 21,* April 1905 - March 1906, p. 24; *Vol. 43,* January 22-September 22, p. 153.

Auction Catalogue, UA, Dated November 3 - December 1, 1900.

Bacon, Francis. *Essays and New Atlantis,* Walter J. Black (New York: 1942; "Of Beauty" p. 180-181; "Of Gardens", 190-191. (English gardening theory - 17th century).

Birren, Faber. *Color and Human Response.* Van Nostrand Reinhold Co. Inc. (New York: 1978)

_____. *Color Psychology and Color Therapy: A Factual Study of the Influence of Color on Human Life.* Kissinger Publishing. (New York: 1950, 1961).

_____. *Principles of Color: A Review of Past Traditions and Modern Theories of Color Harmony.* Schiffer Publishing. (Atglen, Pennsylvania: 1987).

Boston Art Guide and Artist's Dictionary. (Re: Boston's Art Schools)..

Boston Blue Book, 1896-1935; especially 1903, 1907, 1928, 1935.

Brown, Marilyn. "The Late Nineteenth Century American Watercolor Manual and Color Theory", unpublished paper, Yale University, 1971.

Browning, Robert. *The Selected Poems of Robert Browning*. Walter J. Black (New York: 1942), "The Lost Mistress" written by Browning to Elizabeth Barrett, his future wife.

_____. *Men and Women*. 2 Volumes, undated.

Bureau of Vital Statistics, Boston, Massachusetts (McCormack Building), "Certificate of Death of Laura Coombs Hills", 1952.

Burke, Edmund. *A Philosophical Inquiry into the Origins of Our Ideas of the Sublime and the Beautiful*. In *The Harvard Classics, Vol. 24*, ed. By Charles Eliot, LL.D., P.F. Collier and Sons, Corp. (New York: 1909.)

Byron, Lord (George Gordon). *Byron*. Undated (antique book, initial page lost).

Cennini, Cennino d'Andrea. *The Craftsman's Handbook*. Trans. By Daniel V. Thompson, Jr. Dover Publishing. (New York: 1933).

Chase, Jr. Eastman Gallery. Exhibition Catalogues re: Pastel Exhibitions of Laura Coombs Hills, 1889-1946, esp. "Seven Pretty Girls of Newburyport."

Chase, William Merritt. Records: "The Pastel Society." Archives of American Art, Boston.

Chevreul, Michel Eugene. *The Principles of Harmony and Contrast of Colors and Their Application to the Arts*. (Based on the 1st English edition, as translated from the 1st French edition), Edited by Faber Birren. Schiffler Publishing. (West Chester, Pennsylvania: 1987).

Chicago Evening Post, Art World. "Wins Miniature Prize", February 7, 1928.

Christian Science Monitor. "Laura Coombs Hills Shows at the Guild of Boston Artists", November 25, 1947.

City of Boston. *Directory. 1913-1914.*

Clement, Clara. *Women in the Fine Arts, 1904.*

Commins, Saxe and Linscott, Robert N., Eds. *The World's Great Thinkers: Man and the State: The Political Philosophers.* Random House. (New York: 1947).

_____. *The World's Great Thinkers: Man and Spirit: The Speculative Philosophers.* Random House (New York: 1947).

_____. *The World's Great Thinkers: Man and Man: The Social Philosophers.* Random House (New York: 1947).

_____. *The World's Great Thinkers: Man and the Universe: The Philosophers of Science.* Random House (New York: 1947).

Copley Gallery, Exhibition Catalogues. "Pastels of Flowers" dated November 22 - December 11, 1926; November 19-December 8, 1928; November 17-December 6, 1930; November 16-December 5, 1931.

Corn, Wanda. *The Color of Mood: American Tonalism 1880-1910.* (San Francisco: 1972).

Craftsman Magazine. "The House That Has the Quality of An Old Homestead: Built By Laura Coombs Hills at Newburyport". UD, UA.

Currier, John. *The History of Newburyport, Massachusetts, 1864-1901.*

Doll and Richards, Exhibition Catalogues. "Pastels of Flowers" dated November 9-28, 1936; November 8-27, 1937; November 7-26, 1938; November 13-December 2, 1939; November 12-27, 1940.

Duncan, Frances. "The Miniatures of Miss Laura Coombs Hills", International Studio, Vol. 41, August 1910, p. XLVI, XLVIII.

Dunlap, William. *History of the Arts of Design in the United States, Volumes I, II - P1, II-P2.* Dover Publications. (New York: 1969).

Elliot, Charles W. *Prefaces and Prologues to Famous Books, Vol. 39.* P. F. Collier and Son, Corp. 1938: "Prefaces to Various Volumes of Poems", William Wordsworth, p. 267-311; "Essay to Supplementary Preface", Wordsworth p. 311-388; "Preface to Leaves of Grass", Walt Whitman, p. 388-410. Various excerpts from *Vol. 41.*

_____. *English Poetry. Vol II, Collings to Fitzgerald.* P.F. Collier & Sons,., (New York: 1938) 465-958.

_____. *The Harvard Classics. French and English Philosophers: Descartes, Voltaire, Hobbes. Vol. 34* P.F. Collier and Son, Corp. (New York: 1938).

Essex County Courthouse. (Last Will and Testament, codicils for Laura Coombs Hills.

Fielding, Mantle. *Dictionary of American Painters, Sculptors and Engravers.* 1926.

Fine Arts Society of London. Archival Records.

Fuller, Lucia Fairchild. "Modern American Miniature Painters". Scribner's Magazine, 1920.

Gerdts, William. *American Impressionism.* Henry Art Gallery, 1980.

Guild of Boston Artists. Archives of American Art, Boston. Catalogue of Exhibitions. "Pastels of Flowers" (of Laura Coombs Hills) dated: November 23-December 5, 1942; November 27-December 9, 1944; November 29-December 18, 1943; November 26 - December 15, 1945; November 18-30, 1946; November 17-December 6, 1967. Boston Herald Newspaper, art editorial.

Guild of Boston Artists Records. Archives of American Art, Boston.

_____. AE. Transcript, May 1915.
_____. AE. Journal, May 4, 1915.
_____. AE. Providence Journal, May 1915.
_____. AE. Boston Herald, March 7, 1915.
_____. AE. UP re: Miniature Exhibition, May 1915.
_____. AE. Boston Herald, May 2, 1915.
_____. AE. Record, November 18, 1914.
_____. AE. Sunday Post, UD.
_____. AE. UP, Two reviews re: Annual Exhibitions: one UD; one dated March 29, 1943.
_____. AE. UP dated 1944.
_____. AE. Boston Herald, December 1944.

Gunderson, Maryanne Sudnick. *Dismissed Yet Disarming: The Portrait Miniature Revival, 1890-1930.* Ohio University. (Ohio: 2003).

Hills, Laura Coombs. Personal Letters:

_____. To Mildred Howells, September 26, 1951.

_____. To Mildred Howells, June 13, 1950.

_____. To Mildred Howells, July 29, 1949.

_____. To Mildred Howells, August 1930.

_____. To Mrs. Donaldson, September 4, 1951.

_____. To Mrs. Constable, August 16, 1951.

_____. To Mildred Howells, undated.

_____. From Doll and Richards Gallery, A. G. McKean, responding to inquiry by Hills.

Hills, Laura Coombs. *Miniatures Painted by Laura Coombs Hills, 1889-1939*. Handwritten Journal of completed works in miniature; at Old Newbury Historical Society, Massachusetts.

Hinson, Mary Alice. "The American Pastel Revival: Fashion and Style", Yale University, Unpublished manuscript: referenced in Theodore Stebbins' *American Master Drawings And Watercolors*.

Historical Society of Old Newbury, Newburyport, Massachusetts. Artifacts and personal effects of Laura Coombs Hills.

Hobbes, Thomas. *Leviathan, Parts I and II*. Bobbs Merrill Company, Inc. (New York: 1958).

Holt, Elizabeth Gilmore. *The Classicists to the Impressionists: Art and Architecture of the Nineteenth Century*. Doubleday. (New York: 1966).

Hume, David. "Of the Standard of Taste" in Charles Elliot's *English Essays, Sidney to Macauley, Vol. 27* Harvard Classics Series, P.F. Collier and Son (New York: 1937).

Isham, Samuel. "The Modern Portrait Painters", *History of American Painting*. MacMillan Company. (New York: 1927), p. 534-537.

Jewett, Sarah Orne. "The Hilton's Holiday" in Kielty, Berardine, ed., *A Treasury of Short Stories*. Simon and Schuster. (New York: 1947), p. 263-275.

Kelleher, Diane. *Research Notes: Laura Coombs Hills, 1977.*

_____. "Chronology: Laura Coombs Hills", research paper, 1978.

_____. *Lilian Westcott Hale: Research Notes, 1978.*

_____. "Style and Stylish Women" in Enchantment: The Art and Life of Lilian Westcott Hale, unpublished manuscript 1978, 1987.

King, Pauline. Century Magazine, "American Miniature Painting", 1900.

Lepore, Sandra B. "Breaking the Accepted Rules of Color" in Exhibition Catalogue *Laura Coombs Hills: Portraits from my Garden.* From The Cooley Gallery, Old Lyme, CT; Lepore Fine Arts, Newburyport, Massachusetts; Vincent Vallarino Fine Art, Ltd. New York, New York.

Mann, Dorothea. "Laura Coombs Hills", *Arts and Artists, Vol. 1*, December 1936, Nov. 7.

Manion, Freida. UP "Artist Exhibits Antique Doll", at Historical Society of Old Newbury, Massachusetts.

Nuttell, Grace Alexander. "A Painter of Miniatures", The Puritan, Vol. V, April 1899; in *American Artists, ed., Vol. III, A-Z.*

Obituary. The Boston Globe. "Laura Coombs Hills", February 21, 1952, p. 24; *American Society of Miniature Painters: History of Origins.* (at Knoedler's, Ardeen, National Academy of Design).

Obituary. UP, "Laura Coombs Hills". February 21, 1952.

Obituary. UP. "Laura Coombs Hills, Noted Artist, Dead at 93", February 21, 1952.

Old Newbury Historical Society. Articles, miniatures, pastels, personal effects of Laura Coombs Hills, 1890, Newburyport, Massachusetts.

Pennsylvania Academy of Fine Art. Exhibition Catalogue. "American Miniature Exhibition, 1919.

_____. Exhibition Catalogue. "Fifteenth Annual Philadelphia Water Club Exhibition and Sixteenth Annual Exhibition of Miniatures." UD.

Prang, Louis. *The Chromolithographs of Louis Prang - 1888.* (at the Boston Public Library).

Pratt, Anna. *Flower Talk*. Frederick A. Stokes and Company (New York: 1890); illustrations and mezzotints by Laura C. Hills; at the Boston Public Library.

Pilgrim, Diane H. "The Revival of Pastels in Nineteenth Century America", unpublished, As referenced in Theodore Stebbins' *American Master Drawings and Watercolors*.

Philadelphia Water Color Club. Catalogue. "Fifteenth Annual Exhibition and Sixteenth Annual Exhibition of Miniatures", November 4-December 9, 1912.

Philpott, A. J. "Flower Painting Exhibit Attracts Enthusiasts", Boston Globe, November 23, 1947.

Quigly, Isabel. *Shelley*. Penguin Books (Great Britain: 1956).

Roberts, Eleanor. "Flower Artist at 91 Finds Work Still in Demand - - Has Won Many Medals", Boston Sunday Post, April 8, 1951.

Runge, Clara. "The Tonal School of America", International Studio, Vol. 27, January 1906, (referenced in Gerdts *American Impressionism*, p. 25.

Smith, Henry Nash. *Virgin Land: The American West as Symbol and Myth*. Harvard University Press (Cambridge: 1970).

Smith, Page. *Daughters of the Promised Land*. Little, Brown. (Boston: 1970).

Smith, Ralph C., *Biographical Index of American Artists*.

Spaulding, Florence. *Art and Artists*. Ed. Dorothea Lawrence Mann, published by a "group of Members of the Boston Art Club", Vol. I, December 1936, No. 7.

Stebbins, Theodore E. *American Master Drawings and Watercolors: A History of Works on Paper from Colonial Times to the Present*. Harper and Rowe Publishers. (New York: 1976).

Time and the Hour, "Famous People at Home", May 22, 1897.

Van Rensalear, M. G. "American Painters in Pastel", Century Magazine, December 1984, p. 207; As noted in Stebbins *Master Drawings*.

Vose, Robert C. Speech. "Laura Coombs Hills" delivered at Old Newbury Historical Society on the occasion of the 100th anniversary of the birth of Laura Coombs Hills.

Waters, Clara. *Artists of the Nineteenth Century and Their Works.* (Boston: 1885)

Whitman, Walt. *The Selected Poems of Walt Whitman.* Walter J. Pach (New York: 1942).

Williams, Alyn. "Royal Society of Miniature Painters in England", July 1924. UP.

Williamson, G. C. and Buckman, P., RMS (Royal Miniature Society) *The Art of the Miniature Painter.* Chapman and Hall, Ltd. (London: 1926), "Miss Laura Hills of Boston, U.S.A.", p. 238.

Who's Who in American Art, Vol I-1936; Vol.II-1938; Vol. IV-1947.

Who's Who in New England, 1916, 1938.

Women in the Fine Arts, UP, p. 162.

* Note: Many tidbits of research information came to me in bits and pieces, with only partial notations for sources, so some individual entries in this bibliography may be incomplete.

About the Author

Born and educated in Massachusetts, Miss Kelleher began her undergraduate studies in the Liberal Arts at prestigious Wheaton College in Norton, where she was on the Dean's List. A transfer student, she received the degree of "Bachelor of Arts with Distinction" from Simmons College, Boston. Graduating in the top five percent of her class while majoring in Sociology, Economics and Art History, beyond "Distinction" additional baccalaureate honors conferred included: Academy (Collegiate Honor Society), Departmental Recognition (History of Art), Dean's List and receipt of academic grants.

Further general art historical studies and specialized new directions reflecting a burgeoning interest in American Art and Culture as well as European Painting of the Nineteenth Century, were undertaken within the Department of the History of Art, Master of Arts and Doctor of Philosophy program at Boston University's Graduate School of Arts and Sciences. By age twenty-four, she had independently researched and authored her first book and the first art historical book ever written on Boston artist, Lilian Westcott Hale - titled *Enchantment: The Art and Life of Lilian Westcott Hale, America's Linear Impressionist*. A year later came the independently researched and written *Unlikely Icon* and the majority of *Sense, Sensibility and Sensation: The Marvelous Miniatures and Perfect Pastels of Laura Coombs Hills, America's Lyrical Impressionist*.

Eventually, new interests in English Literature beckoned, so Kelleher completed a Master of Arts Degree in English Literature at Clark University in Worcester, Massachusetts, where she received a full scholarship and wrote her book *The Rose Upon the Trellis: William Faulkner's Lena Grove*.

Currently enrolled in the Master of Science Degree in Business Administration at Worcester State University, Kelleher is pursuing business courses while editing her soon-to-be-published book on Laura Coombs Hills. She was also accepted to study at Clark University, having received the Clark Alumni Scholarship.

Her other five books include: *The Fantasmagorical Feline Adventures of Little Miss Libby; The Secrets of Willow Creek; How to Research, Write and Publish an Art History*

Book in American Art; and *Unlikely Icon: The Art, Culture and Philosophy of Forest Hills Cemetery, Boston: A Nineteenth Century Symbol of American Values* and *A Brief Book of Children's Tales.*

She is the niece of the renowned Hollywood writer and producer, the late Paul W. Keyes of Paul W. Keyes Productions, Westlake Village, California.

Printed in the United States
by Baker & Taylor Publisher Services